STEPN
OWN
RAILWAY

A History of The London & Blackwall System

By J.E.Connor

Published by

Connor & Butler

69 Guildford Road, Colchester, Essex CO1 2RZ.

To My Son Charlie

Who although still young in years
has already acquired a wide knowledge
of his father's subject.

Contents

Second Edition 1987
Typesetting: Connor & Butler.
Proofs checked by P.A.J.Perris.
Cover design, maps and general graphics by J.E.Connor.
Printed by the Owl Printing Company, Tollesbury, Essex.

ISBN 0 947699 08 2

INTRODUCTION

One of my earliest memories is being held up by my mother to watch a grubby old tank locomotive shunting wagons along the viaduct at the bottom of Salmon Lane. I must have been only around a year old at the time, but for some reason, the event has printed itself indelibly on my mind. I can recall being sat on one of the canal bridge bollards, and being told to wave at the driver, but whether he waved back or not, I'm afraid I didn't notice. At the time I think I was too busy gazing up at the engine itself, and wallowing in the appetising aroma which was wafting over from a nearby turtle soup factory. Stepney in the post-war era was a vastly different place from what it is now, and everything seemed wondrous to the eyes of a toddler.

We used to go to Canvey Island a lot in those days, and of course we always took the train. On most occasions we went from Stepney East, but sometimes we would use Fenchurch Street. I vaguely remember the three closed stations along the route, although the only one which I actually knew the name of at the time was Burdett Road. Both Leman Street and Shadwell always looked dark and eerie, but in retrospect I don't suppose they really were. Because I used to find their gaunt broken windows and sinister black waiting rooms a bit disturbing, I tried not to look out at them as our train went by, although this strange trepidation never seemed to apply to Burdett Road. Why this should be I really don't know, but I suppose young children acquire phobias about the most unlikely things.

Sometime before I started school, I remember standing at a bus stop in Burdett Road, and watching the demolition men up on the old station. I don't think that there was too much left of it at that time, although part of the gents urinal remained standing. Typical no doubt of a silly little boy's sense of humour, I thought it was extremely funny when I saw one of the workmen using this, and I think my Mum was a bit embarrassed by my non-stop giggling!

As I grew older, so my interest in railways began to blossom, but it wasn't until the mid-Sixties that I fell under the spell of the lines in my own area. This was a great pity really, because by that time it was all a bit too late, and many of the old structures had disappeared for ever.

Bow Road was still standing however, and I regularly used to look up at this on my way home from school. From the street it was possible to see the old 'Way Out' sign on the down-side stairway, and this hung at an angle as though someone had given it an almighty wallop. Back in the dim and distant past, I vaguely remember the station nameboard still in-situ above its former entrance, but as this must have been a few years after closure, I could well be mistaken.

Over the years I watched the former Blackwall branch deteriorate, and the scheme to include it as part of the new Docklands Light Railway took me by complete surprise. This venture is not only exciting, but from a nostalgic point of view, it's nice to know that the old familiar viaducts, which have existed for nearly 150 years, will be retained for future generations.

I know that much has been written about the line in the past, but the majority of this seems to centre around the archaic rope-hauled period of the 1840's. What I have tried to do is present a complete picture of the system, from its troublesome beginnings through to the present day, and I believe that a great deal of the information included in this book has never been published before.

I must admit that I was somewhat daunted by the prospect of having to set out the whole story in a readable manner, but thanks to the encouragement of a few good friends, I was eventually talked into it, and I hope the result is worthwhile.

My intention from the outset has been to produce a book which will be of interest to Londoners in general, and not just dedicated enthusiasts. Because of this, I have endeavoured to avoid the use of too many over-technical railway terms, although in some cases, this just hasn't been possible. However, I have done my best to ensure accuracy.

In choosing the photographs for the book, I have tried to find as much unusual material as possible, and not fall back on those which have appeared in other publications. This has been quite difficult since the line seems to have attracted little attention from photographers and views of it are hard to come by. I am always interested in finding out more about the railway and would be delighted to hear from readers who remember it, especially if they have pictures of stations and associated structures or indeed surviving tickets or other artifacts relevant to its history.

As this work is intended for the general reader, I have not included detailed sources of reference, as these can often confuse the flow of the narrative. However, I have compiled a list of useful publications which can be found at the end of the book.

For assisting me with my researches, I would like to thank Chris Lloyd and Harry Watton of the Tower Hamlets Local History Library in Bancroft Road, Tom Ridge of the Ragged School Museum Trust in Copperfield Road and David Sexton of the Docklands Light Railway, all of whom have given invaluable help.

I would also like to thank everyone else who has assisted in any way, especially Barbie for giving me the inspiration, and Tricia for putting up with all the late nights and checking the proofs.

This then is the story of Stepney's Own Railway, I hope that everyone who reads it finds the line as fascinating as I always have.

J.E.Connor
September 1987

This portion of the Sheet is to be detached from the Warrant and retained for the information of the Proprietor.

London and Blackwall Railway Company.

No. **204**

Secretary's Office, Fenchurch Street Terminus.
(Chief Entrance: John Street, Crutched Friars, London, E.C. 3.)

30th December, 1922.

Proprietor Marion S. Grieveson

I am desired to forward you the above Warrant for the Interest for the Half-year ending 31st December, 1922, upon the Debenture Stock of this Company, of which you were registered as the Proprietor on the 16th instant, when the Transfer Books were closed, viz.:

	£	s.	d.
On £ 1500 Stock at £4 5s. per cent. per annum	31	17	6
Less Income Tax at 5s. in the £	7	19	5
Amount to be paid £	23	18	1

I hereby certify that the amount of Income Tax deducted from this Interest has been retained out of the rent payable by the Great Eastern Railway Company, as Lessees of this undertaking.

S. [illegible] SAVAGE, Secretary.

N.B.—The Inland Revenue Department will receive this Statement as a Voucher on claiming repayment of Income Tax, and where the Proprietor is entitled to claim exemption or abatement, this portion of the Sheet must be preserved for the purpose.

9568 11 22

IN THE BEGINNING

The first plans for a type of railway to link Blackwall with Central London were formulated as long ago as 1825. To speed up the transportation of goods from the docks, a scheme was devised to lay an iron tramway on the Commercial Road along which wagons could be hauled by horses, or cables attached to strategically placed winding engines. Although the Bill received two readings in the House of Commons, support was deemed insufficient and Parliament finally rejected it in 1828.

Commercial Road had been built at the beginning of the Nineteenth Century as a broad thoroughfare which provided direct access from the City to the newly opened East and West India Docks, and its trustees levied tolls at certain points along its route. Naturally they were concerned about the possible loss of revenue that might follow the opening of a competing railway, and when a similar project was announced in the mid-1830's, many meetings were organised to sway local opinion away from the idea. Between 1827 and 1829, they constructed a stone 'tramway' along the length of their road, and this they claimed, dispensed with the need for any other form of transportation. It consisted of a double line of Aberdeen granite slabs, which were set into the road surface to form a kind of track. This made the carts run more smoothly, and therefore reduced the labour of the horses that were pulling them. The vehicles that used it all had to have their wheels set to the appropriate gauge, and they were known to the authorities as 'Caravans'. The cost of cartage charged to the users of the tramway worked out at four shillings per ton, and this included the customary toll fee. George Parker Bidder was one of the engineers responsible for its construction, and in the years that followed, he became very instrumental in the planning of the line which later became known as the London & Blackwall Railway.

Promoters continued to seek authorisation for a proper railway to serve the district, and on the 21st of March 1836, a Parliamentary Committee began the task of sifting through the evidence, both for and against its construction. After nearly four months, their work was completed, and their findings were announced on the 17th of June.

One of the main arguments for the provision of the line was based

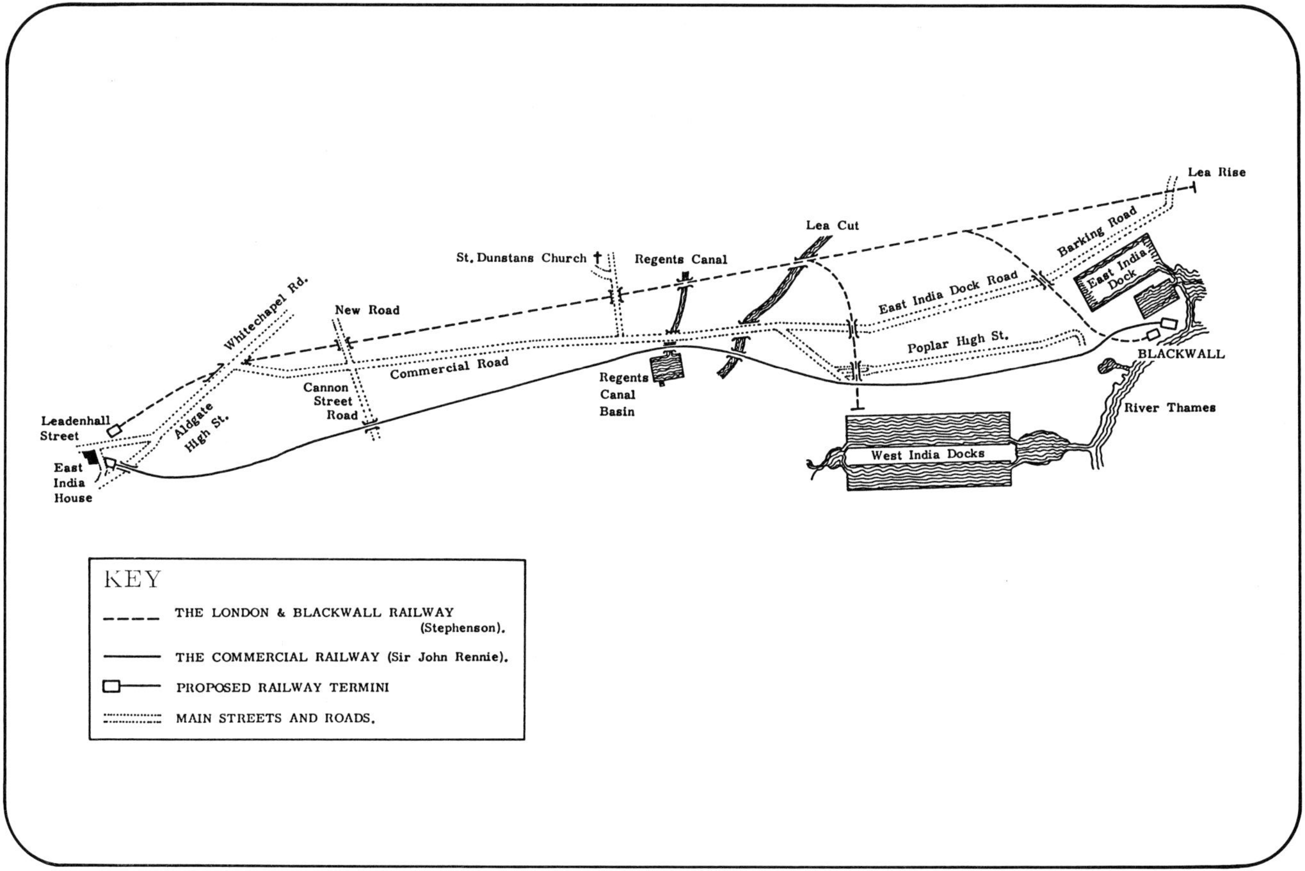

THE TWO PROPOSED RAILWAY ROUTES BETWEEN THE CITY AND BLACKWALL.

upon the congestion caused by shipping in the Pool of London. This had increased drastically in a comparatively short time, and whereas only around 11,000 vessels had entered the Pool during 1796, this grew to over 25,000 in 1835. On a normal day, between the hours of 8 am and 8 pm, an average of 96 steamers passed Limehouse Reach, to which were added a vast number of small craft such as lighters and rowing boats. There was a ruling that a clear lane of 300 ft. was to be left in midstream, but nevertheless traffic jams regularly occurred, and these took many hours to sort out. Boats were unloading passengers and goods, both at the wharves and into small ferries, and the scene at the time must have been very busy indeed.

As early as 1815, the first passenger-carrying steamboat made its debut on the Thames, and within a few years, the river was in constant use by such vessels throughout the holiday season. Steamers operated eastwards from the City to Gravesend, as well as to the various seaside resorts of Kent and Essex. For around fifteen years the number of boats employed on these services multiplied enormously, and although the fares were undoubtedly very competitive, the aspect of safety was inclined to be overlooked by many of the proprietors. Often in the absence of a proper landing stage, a company would erect a makeshift pier by planking over a row of old barges, and the passengers had to negotiate such dangerous contraptions when joining or leaving their craft. Evidence was given to the Committee of the many fatal accidents to river users, caused when small boats were capsized and swamped by the swell of larger vessels. The journey time by river to Blackwall was also rather a lengthy one, and the 6½ mile trip from St. Katherine's Dock took over an hour.

At the Inquiry it was claimed that the water at Blackwall was deep, and the 750 ft. long quay which was then owned by the Company of Messrs. Green Williams and Green, was capable of taking seven of the pleasure craft at any one time. It was therefore an ideal place for ships either to start or terminate, and thus avoid the congestion further upstream. The argument was also forwarded that the proposed railway would be of great commercial value by serving the various docks in the area.

The distance along Commercial Road from the City to Blackwall was almost 3 miles shorter than the course of the river, and passenger traffic was catered for by horse-drawn omnibuses which ran approximately every five minutes. The fare charged for these was 6d each way, and the journey time was around three quarters of an hour. At the Inquiry, Mr. John Beeton, the proprietor of the East India Dock Tavern, stated that apart from these omnibuses, coaches and 'flies' also called to pick up passengers. The 'flies' that he referred to were light carriages which carried six inside passengers, and three on the outside. All in all, 41 coaches and carriages operated daily from Blackwall, and these were collectively licensed to make nearly 2,000 journeys each week. For the twelve months ending in December 1835, the number of passengers travelling on these was stated to be 1,399,097.

The Inquiry was also told of the quantity of goods that was annually transported between the India Docks and the City, and this amounted to 180,000 tons by land, and about 160,000 tons by water. Taken on average therefore, the total quantity worked out rather more than a thousand tons per working day.

As far as river passenger traffic was concerned, the number of people making the journey between the City and Blackwall was a little less than 3½ million per year, although half of these were only passing through, en-route to a destination further downstream. The quay that was owned by Messrs. Green Williams and Green was known as Brunswick Wharf, and in the mid-1830's it was a very important place for shipping. As well as handling pleasure traffic, it was also the departure point for many emigrant ships to the Colonies, and a port of call for services to the Continent.

There were two different schemes, both with the common aim of building a line to Blackwall. One of these was known as the Commercial Railway, whilst the other had the rather unwieldy title of the London and Blackwall Railway and Steam Navigation Depot. The history of these two projects is rather confusing, as the consulting engineers involved decided to change allegiances whilst the plans were at the formative stage. Initially, the route of the Commercial Railway was surveyed by George and Robert Stephenson, but having done this, they decided to support the other scheme, and leave the responsibilities of their former organisation to Sir John Rennie. Rennie's father was a famous civil engineer of the first half of the Nineteenth Century, and amongst other things he had been responsible for the construction of the East and West India Docks. The Commercial Railway proposed to build their line on a brick viaduct, similar to that already constructed on the London and Greenwich Railway. The route to be taken was to the south of Commercial Road, with a City terminus adjacent to East India House in Leadenhall Street. The other scheme took a more northerly course and although it started from approximately the same location, it was routed via Aldgate High Street and New Road, with two suggested branches which would serve the West India Docks and Lea Rise. This particular plan envisaged that the line would be built in a brick cutting, thirty feet deep and twelve feet wide for almost its entire length. Because Stephenson's route was in a more northerly position than the other, the competing companies were referred to as the 'Northern' and 'Southern' lines respectively.

Despite assurances from Robert Stephenson that the sides of his cuttings would be 'elegantly built', his proposal met with a rather cold response, mainly on the ground that the passengers would be deprived of the extensive views of shipping which could be enjoyed with Rennie's scheme.

The Commercial Railway project therefore appeared to be the most likely of the two to meet with success, but unfortunately the City Corporation had no intention whatsoever of allowing the Company to build a terminus within their exclusive square mile. There was a lot of arguing, and Rennie claimed that nothing short of linking Blackwall with Leadenhall Street would satisfy either him or national prestige, but nevertheless, the Authorities held their ground, and the Company were obliged to accept a less conveniently placed terminus in the Minories.

After the committee sat in the House of Commons for 38 days, the Act which authorised the construction of 'The Commercial Railway' received the Royal Assent on the 28th July 1836.

The Act consisted of 221 clauses, and a schedule of the properties which needed to be demolished in order that the line could be built. It prescribed that "Locomotives or other engines" could be used, although any locomotives should be approved by the Commissioners of Woods and Forests to minimise the risk of fire to surrounding properties. It stated:-

"For the better protection of Persons and Property and being on the line of the said railway, every such engine shall have a proper and screened Hood or Cover of Wire Gauze (the width of the spaces between the Wires of which shall not be more than One-Eighth of an inch from the other) affixed upon the Top of the Shaft of the Chimney thereof."

Apart from the adjoining houses, the greatest risk of fire was considered to be the many sailing vessels which used the Regents Canal Basin, close to the site of the line. The great mass of ships' timbers, rigging and sail-cloth could easily become transformed into an inferno should it be caught by any sparks or cinders emitted from a passing engine. Unfortunately in 1836, the only viable alternatives to steam locomotives were cable haulage or horse traction, and the latter was deemed too slow for the kind of railway that the promoters had in mind. When Robert Stephenson addressed the 1836 Parliamentary Committee, he insisted that because of the value of the property adjacent to the line, the idea would be best forgotten rather than use locomotives. No doubt this statement from Stephenson came as something of a surprise at the time, as both he and his father had always championed the use of locomotives. Not only that, the pair of them had recently experienced a great deal of trouble with other forms of motive power on the Stanhope & Tyne Railway which had opened in 1834. The route of this system ran from South Shields to Stanhope in County Durham, and throughout its length, it employed just about every form of traction imaginable. There were $10\frac{1}{2}$ miles which were worked by horses, $9\frac{1}{4}$ miles by locomotives, 3 miles of self-acting plane, and finally, 11 miles of cable haulage. Apart from the fact that two people were killed on the first day of operation, when a train broke away whilst on a gradient, the line proved to be generally difficult to work, and if nothing else, it underlined the unreliability of stationary winding engines. With this in mind, it seems likely that by emphasising the potential fire hazards, and insisting on an unreliable form of traction, the Stephensons were hoping to rally support for their own scheme, which by this time was doomed to failure.

The following year the two rival companies joined forces, and the feeling that had been engendered in their struggles was indicated by their mutual agreement that the engineer appointed to actually build the line, should be one that had not been previously employed by either organisation. Therefore both Rennie and Stephenson stood aside, apparently without loss of dignity, and made way for the appointment of Mr.William Cubitt.

The first official meeting of the authorised company took place at The City of London Tavern on Tuesday the 9th of January, 1837, and a great deal of enthusiasm prevailed. In his report to the Board of Directors, William Cubitt stated the following:

"The commencement of this railway at the Brunswick Wharf, the chief landing and shipping place for the large steamers, is judiciously chosen, being well adapted for transport to and from town, of goods and passengers by steamers, to and from all parts of the coast and continent; likewise from its proximity to the East and West India Docks, for the conveyance of merchandise to and from these great depots of foreign produce.

The commencement of the railway at the back of the sheds of the wharf is favourable to the transaction of much business; for, by extending their length, the facilities for receiving and discharging passengers will be increased, to which purpose the present sheds may be made available; for to whatever extent they may be carried, the same simple arrangement will hold good,- of one end appropriated to arrivals, and the other to departures, without any crossing or confusion, let the numbers offering be ever so great.

Commencing at a height of clear eighteen feet, the railway crosses, without interruption, the road leading to the Brunswick Hotel and Wharf, and proceeds on arches in the form of an elevated viaduct, with a gradual rise of 1 in 440, or twelve feet per mile, over fields, streets, lanes, roads, canals, and water courses, without interfering with any; and by means of easy and unobjectionable curves, avoiding all property of a very valuable or peculiar description, it passes through a neighbourhood consisting chiefly of houses of the lowest and poorest description to its terminus at the Minories."

From his report, it appears that Cubitt intended for the line to be carried on viaduct for its entire length, but later changes in policy ruled this out. He also suggested that some of the arches could be fitted out as houses, and stated:-

"So far as practicability goes, there is no doubt that they be made water tight, the smoke carried off, both light and ventilation provided, and, in short, that they may be converted into more cleanly and comfortable dwellings than four-fifths of those which will have to be taken down."

On the subject of track, Cubitt recommended that the line should be laid to a wider gauge than the standard 4' 8½", particularly as the company had no intention at the time of joining their system to any other railway.

He expressed his opinion thus:-

" I think it will be found ultimately, that a greater width of rail, than that proposed originally, will be more convenient, wherever much business is required to be done at great speed.

When a railway forms no junction with any other railway, nor is likely to do so, the exact width of the rails may be arbitrarily fixed to any gauge, to suit the circumstances or cost, so as to secure as much as possible of the one at the least possible cost of the other."

In his report, Cubitt also referred to a "proposed extension to Leadenhall Street." It was obvious that the Company were still pressing for their real goal of a terminus a lot closer to East India House, and indeed, later in 1837, they applied unsuccessfully for Parliamentary Approval to extend their railway to Lime Street.

Around this time, the engineer George Parker Bidder came onto the scene. He was born in 1806, and from an early age he displayed a natural genius for mathematics. As a child he was regarded as a phenomenon, and his remarkable talent for mental arithmetic soon drew a great deal of public attention. His father, who worked as a stonemason in his native Devon village of Moretonhampstead, made a profitable living for a while, by travelling around the country with his son and exhibiting him as the 'Calculating Boy'. Fortunately for George, his powers attracted the attention of several eminent men, and some of these paid for his schooling, firstly at Camberwell and later at Edinburgh. His education was completed at the University of Edinburgh, where he met and became a close friend of Robert Stephenson. After a short time working with the Ordnance Survey, and an even shorter period as an insurance clerk, he eventually took to engineering, and in 1834 he assisted his friend Stephenson during the building of the London and Birmingham Railway. In 1837, he recommended to the Commercial Railway directors that because of the potential fire hazards and problems associated with locomotives stopping and starting at closely spaced stations, it would be better if the trains were hauled by cables attached to stationary winding engines. These could be positioned at each end of the line, and the system could be operated in a similar fashion to the various rope-worked railways which were then in existence in the north of England. Surprisingly, after their disastrous experiences with the Stanhope & Tyne venture, the Stephensons agreed, and no doubt determined to learn from their previous mistakes, they gave the scheme their full approval. The idea however was so unusual for a passenger carrying railway, that George Stephenson was ridiculed as a 'visionary' when he explained it in the House of Commons.

With the reassertion of the Stephenson influence, William Cubitt quietly faded from the scene, and today he is probably best remembered in the area as the builder of Cubitt Town on the Isle of Dogs.

In his 1837 report, Cubitt had suggested that a track gauge somewhat wider than 4' 8½" might give greater stability for trains travelling at speed, and this idea was taken up by his successors. Therefore, before construction had commenced, the railway's Board of Directors agreed that their line should be built to a gauge of around 5' and their trains would be hauled by cables attached to stationary winding engines. In many respects it seems strange that George Stephenson had anything to do with the scheme after this, as not only was he an outspoken advocate of locomotive power, but he was also normally adamant about the use of 4' 8½" gauge which he himself had set as standard some years earlier.

The railway, which was just over 3½ miles in length, was to be built from the Minories to Brunswick Wharf at an estimated cost of £600,000. It was to run almost parallel with the south side of Commercial Road, and had provision in the Parliamentary Act for branch lines to serve both the East and West India Docks, should this be requested by the dock companies themselves.

Cubitt had visualised that the line would be carried for its entire length on arches, but for financial reasons this idea was abandoned. Instead, only the section between the Minories and West India Dock was built on viaduct, the remainder being on embankment or in cutting. To reduce the amount of demolition required, a proposed width of 45 ft was implemented, except for certain station sites and the suchlike, where the formation would obviously need to be wider.

The building of the viaduct started at the Minories end, and around the same time, work commenced on the erection of the two engine houses. With construction in its early stages, both George Stephenson and George Parker Bidder were officially appointed as the Company's engineers in January 1838, although from contemporary sources it seems likely that Bidder was responsible for most of the work.

At either end of the line a pair of steam winding engines were installed, both lots having been designed by a Mr. Mozer under the direction of Robert Stephenson. The engine house at the Minories was situated beneath the railway, and was basically 72 ft wide by 48 ft long, although the actual length was increased to 69 ft by the extension which accommodated the cable drums. The Minories engines were of the marine condensing type with side levers, similar to those used on steam vessels a few years earlier. They were built by the company of Messrs. Maudsley, Sons and Field, and were equipped with five boilers. Three of these boilers were constructed on the Cornish system, with two internal tubes through their entire length and a furnace at their front end. The other two were of the square marine type with ordinary internal furnaces and rectangular flues. This second pair were equal in power to the three of Cornish design, and both sets were intended to be used alternatively with each other for three months at a time. During their period of inactivity, the set that was not in use was to be cleaned and serviced. These engines realised 115 hp and had flywheels of 17 ft diameter, which by means of cogs, worked the massive 23 ft cable drums.

The engines at the other end of the system were situated beside the line, slightly west of the Blackwall terminus. They were similar in layout to those already described, but were built to a smaller scale. They were constructed by the company of Barnes and Miller, and were again of the marine side-lever type. They had a nominal force of 70 hp each and their $45\frac{1}{2}''$ diameter pistons made an average speed of 25 strokes per minute. The reason that these engines required less power was because the line was built with a slightly falling gradient as it ran eastwards, and Blackwall station was 68 ft lower than its counterpart at the Minories.

As the engines at both termini were only to be worked for 8 or 9 minutes out of every quarter of an hour, it was felt that the vacuum in the condenser might be impaired by leakage whilst the machines were standing idle. As a good vacuum was deemed necessary to enable everything to start promptly, a couple of small 12 hp engines were added to work auxiliary air pumps which helped to maintain the vacuum in the condensers of the main engines.

To reduce the speed of incoming trains, and to give impetus to those that were departing, a short incline of 1 in 150 was provided between the winding engines and the terminus that they served.

Two tracks were provided, and each was supplied with about seven miles of hemp rope. This had a circumference of 5¾" and weighed 8 lb per yard. The ropes were manufactured by the Limehouse firm of Huddart & Co. and cost the Railway a total of £2,891.14s.9d. Each line had a pair of 3'2" wide winding drums, and these were arranged so that as the rope wound around one drum it unwound from the other. In this way there was always about 3½ miles of rope on each drum, whilst the remainder was on the line. Between the engine houses, the ropes ran in cast iron sheaves of 3' diameter, which were spaced 33' apart in the centre of the track. In an attempt to prevent twisting, swivels were later provided at certain intervals along the route, and the track itself was laid with 50 lb rail on wooden sleepers.

From the Minories, the line was carried for the first 4,020 yards on a viaduct which comprised 285 arches. This gave way to an embankment slightly east of West India Dock Road, and the tracks finally descended into a cutting for the final section into Blackwall.

Of the viaduct itself, the majority of the arches were built with a standard span of 30 ft, but the three that bridged the Regents Canal Basin, and the one over the Limehouse Canal, measured 87 ft. The section over the Basin was fitted with an ornamental iron balustrade, supposedly to deaden the sound of passing trains, but rather more likely as an attempt at decoration. Dwellings were built into the arches in Trinidad Street, Limehouse, and a small public house was similarly incorporated in nearby Mill Place. This little establishment was leased to Taylor Walker & Co. who owned the local Barley Mow Brewery.

Five small intermediate stations were planned to serve the various districts along the line. These were to be positioned at Shadwell, Stepney, Lime-house (sic), West India Docks and Poplar, and were to be constructed very simply, using mainly wood.

The two termini were to be somewhat more elaborate, but before too much work had been completed at the Minories, the Company heard that their latest bid for a better sited station had been successful, and that Parliament had agreed to a 415 yard extension into Fenchurch Street. Blackwall was graced by a very fine building indeed, but the one erected at the Minories emphasised the station's temporary nature. It consisted of two platforms nestling beneath a short overall roof, and although its street level frontage was adorned with a little ornamentation, no real enthusiasm was put into the design.

In 1839, at the same time as the extension into Fenchurch Street was approved by Parliament, the Company's title was changed from 'The Commercial Railway' to 'The London & Blackwall Railway', and within a few months the line was ready for opening.

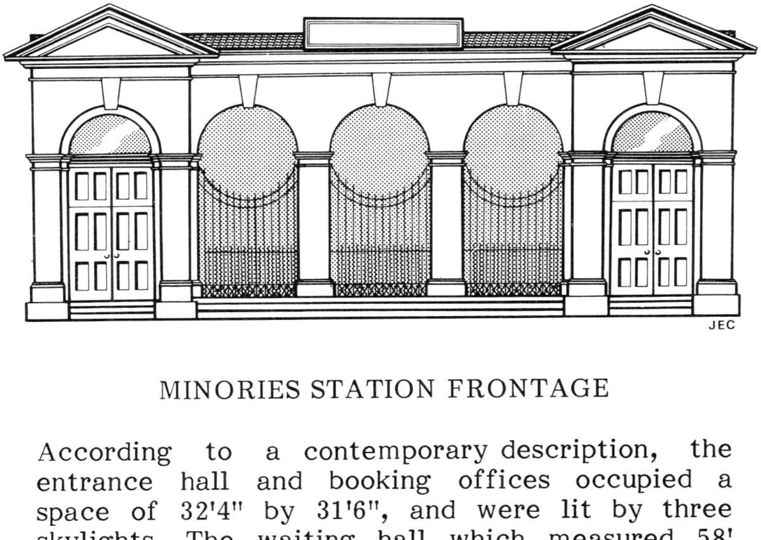

MINORIES STATION FRONTAGE

According to a contemporary description, the entrance hall and booking offices occupied a space of 32'4" by 31'6", and were lit by three skylights. The waiting hall which measured 58' by 56' 8" was divided into First and Second Class by the 10' wide arrival stairs which led down from the platforms.

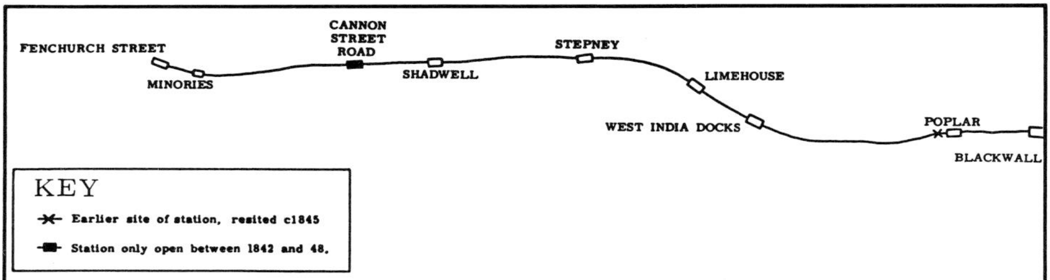

THE LONDON & BLACKWALL RAILWAY 1840 - 1849.

INTERMEDIATE STATION AS ORIGINALLY BUILT
Believed to be Limehouse or West India Docks.

Based on the original architects drawings

THE FOURPENNY ROPE

With only one track in operation, and two of the intermediate stations still under construction, the line was ceremonially opened on Saturday, the 4th of July, 1840. The occasion was typical of the great civic celebrations which delighted the Victorians, and no less than 1,500 guests were invited by the Directors of the Company. A huge crowd gathered at the Minories to cheer the various public figures and their wives as they arrived and entered the station. The whole place was full of people, and there was an air of great excitement as the railway guards in their blue uniforms with white braid trimmings, began to conduct the first batch of passengers to their train. A telegraphic signal was sent to Blackwall to advise the staff that all was ready, and at twelve o'clock, mid-day, to the accompaniment of a brass band, the first set of carriages left for Brunswick Wharf.

Throughout the East End, the route was lined by dense crowds, who cheered and applauded as the train went past. One eye-witness described how the inhabitants of two tenement houses close to the line removed some of their roofing tiles, to enable them to poke their heads through the holes and get a better view of the proceedings.

The first train itself took fifteen minutes to complete the journey, but subsequent ones were rather quicker. Nevertheless, because of the vast number of people, and the limited accommodation available in the coaches, it took several trips to convey all the guests to Blackwall.

At one o'clock, preceded by his sword and mace bearers, the Lord Mayor of London was escorted to his train at the Minories, closely followed by a group of civic dignitaries and their wives. At the other end of the line, passengers who had already arrived at Blackwall, gathered on the broad riverside terrace, and were entertained by the Woolwich Marine Band.

Once the guests had all arrived, the doors of the East India Company's warehouse at Brunswick Wharf were opened at three o'clock, and the banquet commenced. The building had been specially carpeted, and flags were hung from the walls to add a touch of dignity. In a large room on the first floor, Mr. Lovegrove, the owner of the nearby Brunswick Tavern, provided the guests with a gourmet meal which included turtle with iced punch, whitebait with champagne, and grouse with claret. After various lengthy speeches, the festivities were declared to be over, and everyone was at liberty to return to central London. Some of them travelled by the train. Others, who no doubt felt the need for fresh air, decided to go by river, and sailed on the steamboat 'Ariel', which had been chartered from the Woolwich Steam Packet Company.

The following Monday - July the 6th, the line was opened to the general public, and a regular service of trains was inaugurated between the Minories and Blackwall. At first, the only intermediate stations in use were those at Lime-house (sic), West India Docks and Poplar, and these were served by the one set of rails that were operational. The second line was brought into use on the 3rd of August, and on the same date the station at Stepney was opened. Shadwell however, had to wait a little longer for completion, and wasn't actually finished until the 1st of October.

An Early Ticket

The earliest London & Blackwall tickets were simply thin pieces of paper which the clerk tore from a book. First Class issues such as this were printed on a yellow background, whilst Second Class are believed to have been pale blue.

All early tickets were basically flimsy pieces of coloured paper which had to be surrendered by the passengers as they entered their carriage. Because these were collected at the station of origin, some of the booking clerks began to 'work a fiddle' with the ticket collectors, and re-issue the same tickets over and over again. However, once the Company found out about this, they appointed a 'Ticket Master', at a salary of £1 a week, and in this manner the little opening for fraud was eliminated.

The method by which the railway was operated was highly efficient, even if rather weird by modern standards: At the start of a day's work, a train of seven coaches would be waiting at either terminus, and a single vehicle at each of the intermediate stations. With all of these gripped to the rope, the signal would be given over the telegraph, and the engines at both ends of the line would start winding and drawing the carriages towards them. The coaches from the intermediate stations would travel singly towards their respective terminus, followed by the main trains which would deposit the majority of their formation along the way. When these trains were about twenty yards short of their first station, a guard on the last coach would remove a pin from the coupling, release the gripping apparatus from the rope, then allow his vehicle to glide alongside the platform, where he would stop it with his handbrake. Whilst he was doing this, the remainder of the train continued to hurtle down the track, often travelling at around 30 mph, until it approached the next station where the procedure would be repeated. Eventually, the two coaches which had started their journey at the front of the train would arrive at the terminus, having been preceded by the vehicles from the five intermediate stations. In this manner another seven coach formation would be available for the return trip, and the same sequence of events would be set into action. Shortly before reaching the end of the line, the guards would release their rope-gripping apparatuses, and then bring their carriages to a stand at the terminal station platforms.

By working in this manner, there was no need for the rope to stop once the trains had been set in motion, but although it provided a speedy means of getting from one end of the line to the other, it made journeys between intermediate stations impossible without first travelling into one of the termini. Coaches were arranged in the order of the stations which they served. Therefore, when a train was marshalled at the Minories, the last carriage would be for Shadwell, the next one would be for Stepney, and so on through to the leading vehicle which would be for Blackwall. The method of operation actually varied according to the demands that were made upon it during the day, and although a set of six or seven coaches would be regarded as about standard, it wasn't unknown for a train to comprise of over twenty. The time allowed for the through carriages to cover the complete distance was officially 13 minutes, and four trains were diagrammed every hour between 8.30 am and 8.45 pm.

The coaches that were used on the line were all six-wheelers,

West India Docks station shortly after the line was opened.

From a contemporary engraving.

Artist's impression

of a London & Blackwall Railway composite coach.

This drawing is based on an illustration from an unknown source which is in the possession of the Tower Hamlets Local History Library. The original only shows a guard's platform at one end, but as all contemporary descriptions refer to them as being in pairs, a second one has been added. Unfortunately, detailed drawings of the Railway's rolling stock seem to be very few and far between, and this is the best one that has come to light.

and were painted in a deep shade of blue, lined in gold. Each one carried the Company's crest which comprised the City Arms, surmounted by the steamship emblem of the East & West India Docks, encircled by a device which displayed the Railway's title. They initially only consisted of individual First and Second Class vehicles, but Composites were later introduced to handle intermediate traffic. The First Class carriages were 20 ft long, and were provided with four compartments, each of which had seating accommodation for ten people. The Second Class were two feet shorter in length, and were designed to carry seventy standing passengers. From the beginning these were known by the staff and travelling public as 'Stand-Ups', or more occasionally 'Stanhope Stand-Ups'. Typical of the early railway companies' attitude to what they regarded as the 'Lower Classes', the Blackwall Second Class vehicles were basically open wagons with no glazing whatsoever, and only rather a flimsy roof. Despite such discomforts however, the system was an immediate success, and during their first eighty-one days of operation, the trains carried 570,930 people, and earned the proprietors a total of £8,495.

In his book 'Railways of Great Britain and Ireland', published in 1842, Mr. Whishaw described the First Class compartments, in a style which is somewhat reminiscent of 'Mr. Pooter' in the Grossmith Brothers' classic jibe at the Middle Classes, 'The Diary of a Nobody':-

"They are wanting in elbows, which would sometimes be exceedingly convenient to keep one aloof from an unpleasant fellow traveller."

In the same manner he also expressed his horror at,

"...seeing several most respectably dressed persons riding in the Stanhope Compartments, which are intended especially for those who cannot afford to pay for better accommodation."

The bodies of all the coaches had a width of 7'6", and every one was equipped with an extended platform at each end on which rode two guards, or 'Brakesmen' as they were sometimes known. It was the duty of these employees to operate the 'slip gear' and the rope-gripping apparatus, as well as attend to the two lever brakes which were fitted to all vehicles as standard. Slipping was done as previously described, by removing a pin from the coupling whilst the train was in motion, whereas the rope could be picked up or thrown off by means of a simple device activated by a lever.

Rope haulage for passenger trains was unusual but not unique: Until 1844, the climb out of the Euston terminus of the London & Birmingham Railway was deemed to be too much for locomotives then in existence, and winding engines were installed at the top of Camden Bank. However, the London & Blackwall were certainly the only railway in London to rely entirely on this form of traction, and for its day, the method of working exhibited a great deal of ingenuity.

To avoid snatching and damaging the rope, care was taken to start the engines as gradually as possible, and therefore take up any slack that might be present. Once in motion, the train would gradually be accelerated to its full speed. A brake was fitted to each drum, which was not only used to stop it when required, but also to maintain a certain degree of tension on the part of the rope behind the train whilst it was moving. At first these brakes were made of wood, but as this material tended to catch fire with the constant friction, the Company decided to try something else. For a while they experimented with lead, but in the end they settled for copper, which they found to be the most serviceable.

Immediately in front of the winding equipment at either end of the line was a small cell-like room beneath the track, where a man, known to the Company as a 'Clipper' spent his entire working day. His duty was to operate a piece of apparatus which resembled a large pair of wooden shears, and guide the moving rope neatly onto the drum without it crossing or knotting. The conditions that he suffered must have been almost unbearable, and he had to stand in his subterranean cavern with his arms elevated, all the time that the trains were in motion. The only natural light that entered the room came from a hole in the top, through which he could also have the doubtful pleasure of watching the undersides of the carriages as they trundled above his head. This coupled with the constant muscular strain of guiding the ropes, must have made the 'Clipper's' job one of the most undesirable that the Company could offer.

The efficient operation of the line was totally reliant on the electro-magnetic telegraph which had been newly invented by William Forthergill Cooke and Professor Wheatstone. The idea behind its development was conceived by Cooke whilst studying at Heidelburg in Germany, and on his return to England in 1837, he and his partner immediately had it patented. By today's standards it may seem rather primitive, but in the early 1840's it was the wonder of the age. The wires employed were of copper, enclosed in an iron tube: each wire being separated from its neighbour by some non-conducting material. A much smaller number of needles to denote the required signals were used than in previous telegraphic instruments, and the invention was a vast improvement on any of its predecessors. The temporary magnetism excited by the current in soft iron, rung an alarm bell, and by veritable machinery, a reciprocal arrangement made it suitable for a long line of communication. At one terminus, five needles were arranged with their axes in a horizontal line. When at rest these needles hung vertically, by reason of a slight preponderance given to their lower ends. At the other terminus, five pairs of finger keys, resembling those on a piano, were placed over a trough of mercury to which a battery was attached. On depressing the respective keys, the wires belonging to them made contact with the trough, and received a magnetic current which caused the needles to deflect at the other terminus. Letters of the alphabet were indicated by the movements of the needles, and a definite communication could thus be made between the two points. The instruments at the termini were also rendered reciprocating, with a set of keys and a battery at each station, which enabled either of them to transmit or receive a signal. Originally, the invention only allowed simple signals to be transmitted, but two men employed by the railway during its early days developed a code by which they could correspond and send personal messages from one end of the line to the other. When their actions were discovered by the Line's Superintendent, they were threatened with dismissal, but the Company's officials were so impressed with the code which the men devised, that they were allowed to keep their jobs. The London & Blackwall was the first complete public railway to used the Cooke and Wheatstone electro-magnetic telegraph, and one of the original instruments is now preserved in the Science Museum at South Kensington.

When the line was first opened, the fare charged for a single journey, regardless of station of origin or destination, was 6d for a First Class seat or 3d for a Second Class standing place. The latter was increased to 4d from the 1st of October 1840, and the railway began to be known by the nick-name of 'The Fourpenny Rope'.

Although the idea of rope haulage appeared to be fine in theory, it proved to be very troublesome in practice. The hemp rope that was used initially had a tendency to twist, and this led to an early breakage about a month after the line was opened. When it snapped, the recoil was so violent that it caused a great deal of damage both to the trackwork and a section of the viaduct's parapet near Limehouse. After several experiments with different grades of rope, the Company decided to employ a 1¼" diameter metallic cable, supplied by Messrs. Newall of Gateshead. This consisted of six wire strands around a hempen core, and weighed about 10 lb per fathom.

Unlike their predecessors which had a life expectancy of a month or so, the new cables generally lasted for about a year before they snapped, but of course when they did, the traffic was heavily disrupted. Sometimes, when a cable broke, the passengers were asked to step down from their carriage and assist the guard in pushing the vehicle to the next station, whilst the necessary repairs were being made. Whether these luckless helpers were enticed from the comparative luxury of the First Class accommodation, or else summoned from a meagre 'Stand-Up' is unfortunately not recorded! On one occasion, half way between Shadwell and Stepney, the rope jammed and caused a train to come to a sudden halt in the middle of a wintry blizzard. A couple of hours passed before the apparatus could be persuaded to work, and the passengers, who were mainly sailors travelling back to their ship in the West India Dock, reputedly passed the time by playing snowballs along the track.

Still very much with an eye towards the river traffic as a source of revenue, the Company reached an agreement which allowed them to rent the pier at Brunswick Wharf. By this time the premises were actually owned by the East & West India Docks Company, which had been formed in 1838 when the two independent organisations were amalgamated. The Railway's main aim was to obtain a share of the profits then being made by the steamers which operated the services to Gravesend and beyond. In those days, Gravesend was surprisingly popular during the holiday periods, due mainly to the fashionable Rosherville Pleasure Gardens, which were situated on the outskirts of town. During the 1830's there was an estimated 1,750,000 passengers a year travelling to Gravesend, Margate and Ramsgate, and this was a cake that the Railway dearly wanted a slice of.

As the Company themselves were not authorised to operate their own shipping services, a number of directors grouped together and arranged for the local firm of Ditchburn and Mare to build three iron ships which they intended to use for the Gravesend trips. These entered service between 1841 and 1842, and were named 'The Blackwall', 'The Brunswick' and 'The Railway'. The journey time in 1841 between Blackwall and Gravesend was around seventy minutes when sailing with the tide, and an hour and three quarters when sailing against it. There were six return trips each day, and the fares charged for passengers joining at Blackwall were approximately one-third less than those on other services which originated further upstream.

Another source of income gained from collaboration with river operators was obtained by running trains which connected with the short sailings to Woolwich. In fact, the relationship between the Railway and the ferry owners became so good that by 1844, through tickets to Woolwich began to be issued from all the stations along the line.

The Railway's terminus at Blackwall was a fine piece of architecture, and a contemporary article which appeared in 'The

Mirror' 2d magazine on Saturday 27th March 1841 describes it perfectly:-

"Its general arrangement is pleasing and highly creditable to the taste of the designer, Mr. Tite, architect of the New Royal Exchange, and of this Railway. The elevation consists of a rusticated basement, and an upper floor with five windows, which is crowned by a bold block cornice of Roman Doric character. The basement has square-headed compartments, which are entirely filled with windows resembling Venetian ones. The upper windows have triangular and segmental pediments alternately, and also rustic blocks on their jamb-mouldings. In addition to this principal centre structure (which measures 105 feet in length by 45 feet in height, and is chiefly executed in Portland Stone), there are wings on either side which considerably recede from it. Each of these wings consists of nine arches, making the entire frontage to the river about 400 feet. The centre building contains, on the ground floor, a spacious pay office, besides the convenient waiting rooms, and others for the police; while the whole of the upper floor, with the exception of two waiting rooms, is appropriated to a warehouse for the examination of steam-boat goods. The wings contain the arrival and departure sheds, comprising three lines of rails and covered by a light iron roof; the arches are filled with doors of imitative oak, with upper panels of plate glass, and they communicate with the adjoining wharf."

Although this description quite rightly credits William Tite as the building's designer, it seems likely that the basic layout and general dimensions of the structure were devised by Robert Stephenson, and that Tite was only really responsible for its architectural detail.

The same article in 'The Mirror' magazine also revelled in the delights of dining out at Blackwall, after being 'wafted' down from the City by train:-

"...Nor must we omit to notice the contiguity to the celebrated tavern of the same name, 'a locality of high repute among the city Apicii and connoisseurs in gastronomy', says the 'Companion to the Almanac'; to which we may add, that such repute extends far west of Temple-Bar, and alike attracts to this neighbourhood the gourmand and the gourmet, to enjoy its peculiar delicacy of whitebait, with the luxurious accompaniment of cold punch. And thither, by aid of the Blackwall Railway, he may be wafted in less than 10 minutes! What a delightful association of otium cum rapiditate! Having arrived at the wharf, or pier, nothing can be more invigorating, or repellent of dyspepsia, than the river breeze to be enjoyed in a few turns

along the esplanade. Quocunque aspicias, all is busy in life. With London the metropolis of the world, on the one hand, and the dockyards that have contributed to this proud position on the other; Greenwich and its magnificent palace hospital; the Thames, its forests of masts, its steamers, and small craft; all before you; and bespeaking with wealth and industry of this great commercial nation..."

It's a good description of how a sector of London's population viewed the line at the time, even if the regularity of the Latin quotations seems a little irksome. The writer's reference to 'Apicii' presumably related to the legendary Apicius who was a famous glutton in the days of Ancient Rome.

On August the 2nd, 1841, at a cost to the Company of £250,000, the short extension into Fenchurch Street was opened to the public.

The new terminus was situated slightly south of the thoroughfare after which it was named, and had its entrance on the east side of a new street called Railway Place. Architecturally, it was basically an enlarged version of the Minories, and had a similar layout with two platforms and a wooden overall roof. Its frontage was attractive if unassuming, and was built of brick under a slate roof. The general design was Italianate, and five tall openings, each topped by segmental arches, led from the pavement into the booking hall. Above these entrances there rose a second storey which displayed a series of five large windows, whilst at either end of the building was positioned a buttressed section with a prominent triangular pediment. It was the first station to be opened within the City boundary, and had the distinction of accommodating the country's first railway bookstall, which was owned by the newsagent, William Marshall.

FENCHURCH STREET STATION FRONTAGE AS ORIGINALLY BUILT

Trains entering Fenchurch Street were released from the rope at the Minories, and then continued towards the platform under their own momentum. Departing trains sometimes had to be pushed by members of the station staff, until they began to roll down the 1 in 150 incline to the winding house where they would be reconnected to the rope. As a sop to the City Authorities, the Company agreed to build the entire section between the two stations completely enclosed, and this included the bridge across the Minories. Here the railway was hidden from the outside world by wooden side walls and sash windows, and the whole lot was covered by an iron and slate roof.

THE MINORIES BRIDGE
From a contemporary engraving.

Originally, the Parliamentary Act which authorised the extension, stipulated that no trains would be allowed to run into the City on Sundays, Christmas Days or Good Fridays, and on these occasions all services would be required to terminate at the Minories. However, when it was reported to Parliament that the line had been built in such a way that it was not possible for passers-by to see it in operation, they hypocritically changed their minds, and the Act was repealed in 1842. Nevertheless, in observance of the hours of worship, the Company never ran any Sunday trains between 10.45 am, and 1.00 pm, either into Fenchurch Street or anywhere else on their system.

1842 was also the year when the Company began to experiment with a small amount of freight traffic, and a little goods depot was built for this purpose at Crutched Friars between the Minories and

Fenchurch Street. The structure itself was only temporary, and consequently rather primitive. There was a siding at which seven carriages could stand, and a platform about 25 ft wide for receiving goods. This platform was fitted with three traps, and one of these had a crane for lowering goods onto the carts in the street below. The other two had connecting chutes for sliding merchandise in bags or bales to an intermediate store, and there were more cranes on the lower storey. A similar establishment was erected beside the line at West India Docks, and a goods hoist was installed at Poplar, but unfortunately the method by which the railway was operated was little suited to the conveyance of freight, and after a few disappointing years the meagre service was abandoned.

Apart from the general lack of interest displayed by the public towards the Company's freight activities, the number of passengers also failed to reach the total that had previously been anticipated, and in an attempt to boost flagging receipts, a new station was opened at Cannon-street Road between the Minories and Shadwell on the 21st of August, 1842. Regrettably however, this did little to improve the immediate financial state of the organisation, and at the end of August the Board of Directors announced that no dividend would be paid to the shareholders for the previous six months.

The biggest disappointment was that the hoped for increase in the number of people using the line in connection with river traffic had not materialised. This perhaps came as some surprise, as more and more ships were beginning to use Brunswick Wharf, attracted by the facilities which were being offered by the Railway. A regular sailing to Antwerp and Rotterdam had just been inaugurated by the Batavia Line, and special boat trains were operated from Fenchurch Street, but nevertheless passenger receipts continued to dwindle. In another attempt to improve profits, the Company decided to increase all fares by an additional 2d, and therefore raise the cost of a First Class ticket to 8d and a Second Class ticket to 6d. These increases applied from the 12th of September, 1842, but proved so unpopular that the fares from intermediate stations reverted back to their old rate from the 3rd of November.

LONDON AND BLACKWALL.

Trains every day to and from London and Blackwall, and the intermediate stations of Cannon-street road, Shadwell, Stepney, Limehouse, West India Docks, and Poplar, every quarter of an hour from ¾ past 8 in the morning, till a ¼ to 9 at Night.

FARES.—To or from London, Blackwall, and Poplar, first class, 8d.; 2nd class, 6d.; to or from the other stations, first class 6d., 2nd class 4d.

London terminus in Fenchurch-street and Minories, and Blackwall terminus at the Brunswick Wharf.

On **Sundays** the trains cease running from 10½ till 1, being the hours of church service.

The horse buses which plodded along Commercial Road were beginning to appear to be stronger opposition than the Company originally expected, and many people still preferred to use these rather than travel on the railway. This was particularly noticeable when it came to traffic between intermediate stations, where the round about journey which was necessary to get from one place to another, made the trains understandably unpopular. After all, who in their right mind would want to travel between the stations at Stepney and West India Docks, if it meant making a lengthy detour to Blackwall or Fenchurch Street en-route? Admittedly, the railway was still a lot faster, but then the buses had the advantage in that they were direct. Because of this, the Directors of the Company decided that the best way to combat the opposition was possibly by offering cheaper fares, and on the 28th of February, 1843, the price of tickets was again reduced. For passengers travelling all the way from the City to Blackwall the cost reverted to the old 6d First Class, and 4d Second Class, whilst the fares between the intermediate stations changed to 4d and 3d respectively. In addition to this, new cheap tickets were offered to those who made bookings for combined rail and river journeys.

The public seemed delighted, particularly as the Company had to stand down after unsuccessfully trying to squeeze more money out of them. For a short while at least, the line again became popular, and a song was even sung in the local music halls which contained the following words:-

"Hi! Ho! Who's for the Bank,
Fenchurch Street and the Blackwall Line.
Hi! Ho! Who's for the Bank,
It's fourpence all the way!"

Unfortunately, despite the general air of approval from the people who used the line, the decision to reduce fares was seen by the Company's shareholders as an unacceptable step, and pressure was therefore placed upon the Directors to resign.

By 1844 however, things were beginning to look up, and during that year upwards of two and a half million passengers were carried. The average receipts were around £100 per day, but the traffic to and from the intermediate stations still failed to improve. The old problem of snapping cables continued to bug the railway, and the Company report of February 1844 mentions no less than six breakages over as many months. By this time many of the people involved were starting to doubt the wisdom of the cable-hauled system, and for a while the Company Directors considered a plan to convert their line to atmospheric working. The following year however, an extension was sanctioned which was destined to change the Blackwall Railway completely.

In January 1845, a Special General Meeting of the Company's shareholders was held at the London Tavern, to authorise an application for Parliamentary Authority to construct a line from their existing station at Stepney through to the Essex Town of Epping. The route to be taken entailed a junction with the Eastern Counties Railway near Bow, from whence the Blackwall Directors proposed to use the other Company's tracks as far as Stratford, and then construct a new line through Wanstead, Woodford, Chigwell, Loughton and Abridge. Not surprisingly, the Eastern Counties objected in the strongest possible terms, and despite an offer from the Blackwall Company that some of the Eastern Counties' trains would be permitted to use Fenchurch Street as a return gesture, they decided not to allow running rights over their line to Stratford. Eventually however, a tenuous agreement was reached between the two companies, which allowed the Blackwall Railway to construct the section between Stepney and the junction at Bow, on the condition that the Eastern Counties had the sole rights to the Epping Scheme.

Like the Blackwall system, the Eastern Counties had originally been built to a non-standard gauge of 5 ft, but this had been altered to 4' 8½" in 1844. The greatest advantage of connecting the two railways was that it gave the Blackwall Directors the excuse that they had been waiting for, to ditch both the idea of cable-haulage, and the abnormal track gauge in one fell swoop. They applied to Parliament for permission to convert their line to one which employed normal locomotives, and Acts were passed in 1845 and 1846 which gave them the necessary authority to go ahead. After five years of twisted, jammed or snapped cables, the end of the rope was at last in sight, and the Blackwall Railway would cease to be an isolated curiosity.

Presumably in connection with the proposed alterations, the original station at Poplar was closed around this time, and replaced by a slightly larger one on the opposite side of Brunswick Street. The old platforms remained in-situ and were later used for other purposes.

Despite its various operating problems, the Company's profits were continuing to improve. The number of passengers carried for the half-year ending the 30th of June 1845, was 1,524,077, and this represented an increase over the previous six months of 46,840 people.

At a meeting of Civil Engineers on the 13th of January 1846, various personalities discussed the difficulties experienced with cable working, both on the Blackwall line and on various minor railways throughout the provinces. Robert Stephenson defended its use, but admitted that he could not find a solution to the problems which caused the rope to twist, whilst George Parker Bidder still spoke highly of the system's potential. He said that on the London & Blackwall it was necessary to start with six carriages on the rope, but sometimes there were as many as twenty-three or twenty-four. The trains that the Company operated often totalled between 100 and 200 tons, whereas the average weight of a locomotive hauled train of the period hardly exceeded 50 tons. All this aside however, Bidder was careful to point out that he was no longer responsible for any actual supervision of the line, and that the problems were no longer his!

Since its introduction back in 1840, there had been no fatalities as a direct result of the railway being cable worked, but this record was marred by a nasty accident which happened in the January of 1848. A guard on a single coach from West India Docks failed to release the grip from the rope as he approached the Minories, and the resulting accident ripped off the vehicle's front-end and threw the unfortunate man under its wheels. He was badly mangled with an arm and a leg totally crushed, and although he was rushed to hospital, he died the following morning. Maybe he had a lapse of concentration and failed to notice where he was, or else the gripping apparatus may have been faulty, but either way we'll never know, and the accident remains a mystery.

With work on the line to Bow progressing steadily, the Company opened negotiations with the recently formed East & West India Docks and Birmingham Junction Railway, regarding the possibility of these newcomers using Fenchurch Street as their City terminus. The new railway had been promoted to provide the London & North Western Company with a direct route from the West Midlands to the India Group of Docks, and although it was primarily intended for freight traffic, its promoters were beginning to think about introducing a local passenger service as well. Initially the line would extend from Islington to Bow, and then continue in a southerly direction to the docks at Poplar, and a south-western direction to a junction with the new Blackwall Extension Railway. Naturally the Blackwall Company were enthusiastic about this proposal, as extra traffic obviously meant an increase in revenue, but in their haste to reach an agreement, they managed to upset the Directors of the Eastern Counties Railway, and any thoughts of Blackwall trains being allowed to run into Stratford had to be shelved.

The completion date for the new line was originally set for the latter part of 1847, but various problems beset the scheme, and the construction work took longer than expected. Firstly, the Company had difficulty in producing an acceptable design for the bridge over Bow Road, and then they found the job of erecting the new

Commercial Road bridge to be rather more lengthy than anticipated.

With all this going on, the service between the City and Blackwall began to suffer, and the Company announced that one of the tracks would have to be closed for a while, to enable its gauge to be reduced to 4'8½". Therefore, in October of 1848, the 'North Line' was taken out of commission to enable the engineers to relay it to the standard width, whilst the service continued on the 'South Line' only, with a train running every half-hour. Shortly afterwards, in November or December, the little used station at Cannon-street Road was permanently closed to all traffic.

The Blackwall Extension Railway, as the new line was called, was due to be opened some time during October 1848, but this was again delayed by the fact that the bridge over Commercial Road was still unfinished. The work was finally completed by the following January, but then another month had to pass whilst the proposal for using locomotives on the original line was approved by the Commission of Woods and Forests. To comply with safety regulations, the entire section of the viaduct beside the Regents Canal Basin had to be hooded with a light iron roof to lessen the danger of any wooden ships being ignited by a stray spark. With this work carried out satisfactorily, the line was declared to be safe, and all was ready for the transformation to locomotives.

The era of cable haulage finally came to an end on the 14th of February 1849, and following this, the redundant equipment on the 'South Line' was disconnected. From the same date, locomotives began working a 40 minute interval service on the 'North Line', and at last the London & Blackwall had become a conventional forward-looking railway. With the demise of the old system, the station at the Minories was felt to be of no further use, and it was closed to all traffic after the departure of the last cable-hauled train. Work on reducing the gauge of the 'South Line' started immediately, and the job was completed by the 31st of March. Two days later, it was brought back into use, and a full service was inaugurated, using both tracks in the standard manner, and providing a train every ten minutes.

Early in the May of 1849, the stationary winding engines were offered for sale at the auction rooms of Messrs. Pullen & Sons, and fetched a total price of £11,710. The pair from the Minories, together with their five boilers were bought for £6,949 and were later installed at the City Corn Mills, where they worked machinery from 1853 onwards.

For the Blackwall Line, the days of isolation were over: with locomotive hauled trains running on standard gauge track, and with the promise of extra traffic by way of the new Extension Line, it was now ready to become an integral part of the fast growing network of London's railways.

GROWING UP

To operate the new services, a series of six small locomotives were ordered from the engineering firm of Jones and Potts, and these were built in 1848. They were all 2-2-2 well-tanks with 5'6" driving wheels and 3'6" carrying wheels. The engines were originally fitted with two $13\frac{1}{2}$"x18" outside cylinders, but these were later replaced by larger ones which measured 14" x 20". Each locomotive weighed around 22 tons, and when not in use they were accommodated in a shed at Blackwall. They were of a design known as 'The Crewe Type', and they must have looked very attractive with their tall copper-capped chimneys, and shining blue paintwork. The Company numbered them 1 - 6, and they were named respectively: 'Stepney', 'Shadwell', 'Blackwall', 'London', 'Bow', and 'Thames'.

Around the time that the Jones and Potts engines first entered service, an additional pair of 2-2-2 well-tanks were ordered from the Hatcham Ironworks of George England & Co. These differed greatly from the others in both size and appearance, and although their design was in some ways typical of their era, they were also rather ungainly. They had little 4'6" driving wheels set about midway along their length of 15', and their two 9" x 12" cylinders were fed by ugly external pipes which led from beneath their domes.

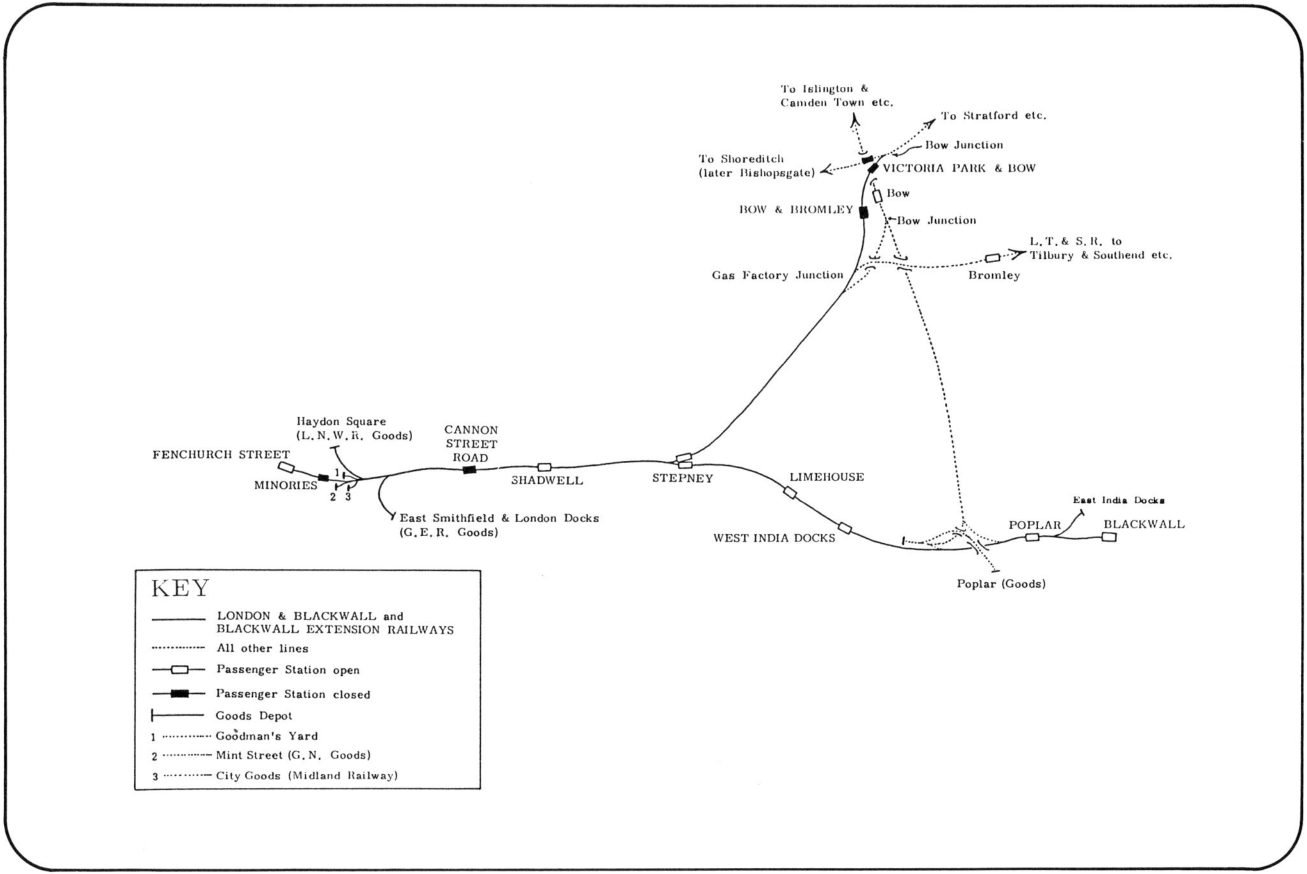

THE LONDON & BLACKWALL SYSTEM 1849 - 1865.

They were much lighter than their counterparts, and weighed only 13 tons, but they were also less reliable, and their stay at Blackwall was destined to be somewhat short. They were named 'Dwarf' and 'Pygmy Giant', and they were purchased by the Company for £1,000 and £950 respectively. The first of these was delivered towards the end of 1849, whilst the second one arrived in the Spring or Summer of the following year. Unfortunately, both of them suffered from various mechanical problems, and therefore after falling into semi-disuse, they were finally sold back to their manufacturers for £700 each, in part-exchange for two new engines.

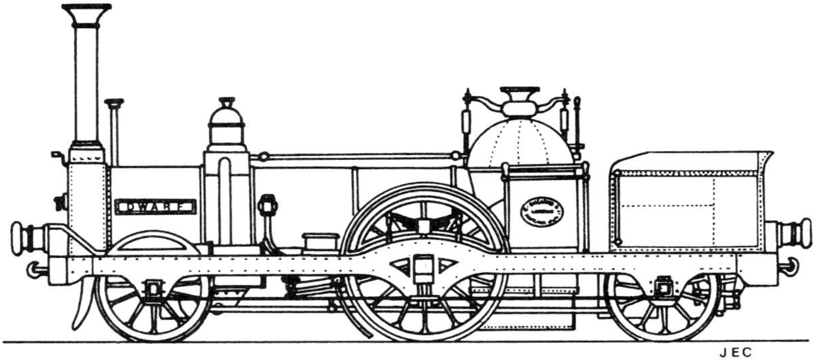

To eliminate the cost of producing new vehicles, the original coaches were converted to run on standard gauge track, and adapted to make them suitable for locomotive haulage. With all this done, they continued in service for well over another decade, until public complaints about their poor condition hastened their demise. During this period they were never fitted with screw-link couplings, and because of this, the vehicles would all start with a jolt as they departed from the station. The effect of this would be most noticeable at the rear of the train, where many of the passengers in the old 'Stand-Up' carriages sometimes lost their foothold and fell to the floor. A retrospective description of such happenings in 'The Locomotive Magazine' for September and October 1904, described the plight of these luckless travellers as 'amusing', and this comment no doubt echoed the contemporary attitude amongst certain members of British society towards those who were unable to pay for the comfort of a First Class seat.

To ensure safety, a system of signalling using flags and lamps was introduced, and the signalman at Stepney was provided with a look-out tower between the two diverging sets of lines.

The early days of the Blackwall Extension Railway were bugged by the bad feeling which existed between the two companies: The London & Blackwall had built the line in good faith, but the Eastern Counties stubbornly refused to have any Fenchurch Street trains running over its tracks. In accordance with the Parliamentary Act which authorised the $1\frac{3}{4}$ mile line, a junction was constructed at Bow, but for a few years this remained unused, and at one time was actually severed by the E.C.R. in a fit of unleashed aggression. An exchange station called Victoria Park & Bow was constructed at the spot where the two companies met, but although this was opened along with the rest of the branch, it was little used, as the E.C.R. refused to provide any connecting services. The majority of the trains which operated over the new line therefore terminated at the flimsy wooden structure which stood on the viaduct to the south of Bow Road. This station's official name was Bow & Bromley, but a few contemporary documents also refer to it as 'Old Ford'. Run-round facilities were provided here for the locomotives, and the only time that a train continued to Victoria Park & Bow was when there was a chance that an E.C.R. train might stop to pick up its passengers.

The bridge which carried the Extension Railway over Commercial Road was perhaps the most impressive piece of engineering on the entire branch. It was constructed by Messrs. Fox, Henderson & Co., to the design of L. Clare, and was of the iron girder type, supported at either end by large brick piers with ornamental capitals. The building of this, together with other structures along the line, was supervised by Joseph Locke M.P., who was one of the Company's directors.

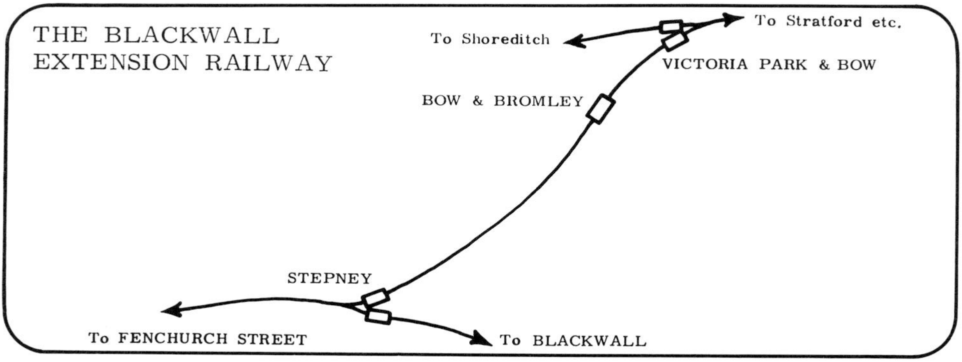

From the 22nd of June, 1849, non-stop trains were introduced on the original line to connect with certain sailings from Brunswick Wharf, and these covered the 3½ miles from Fenchurch Street to Blackwall in five minutes. Other than these, the normal stopping services, which also included the coaches for the branch, took around ten minutes to complete their journey. This included extra station time at Stepney whilst the Bow portion was either detached or attached, depending on the direction of travel. These services were increased from the 11th of August 1849, to provide a train every fifteen minutes, but following a collision whilst attaching some vehicles to an Up working, a shuttle system was introduced on the branch, and passengers using the new line were required to change at Stepney. However, after a number of public complaints about this, the Company agreed to introduce separate through services from Fenchurch Street to Bow, and these commenced to operate half-hourly from the 9th of November 1849. Shortly before this, the directors relented on their previous decision to abandon their premises at the Minories, and on the 9th of September 1849, the old station was re-opened to the public.

The antagonism caused by the hostile attitude of the Eastern Counties Railway finally came to a head, and after the offending company refused to refer the matters in dispute to arbitration, the Blackwall directors were forced to seek Parliamentary assistance. This they duly received in 1850, when the Royal Assent was given to a Bill which ensured the future co-operation of the E.C.R. by instructing them to provide the necessary connecting services, and also to allow through bookings between their stations and places served by the Blackwall line. With the end of these hostilities in sight, the number of trains between Fenchurch Street and Bow were increased to one every fifteen minutes, and the new timetable came into effect from the 18th of March 1850.

Around this time, work was being completed on the new line from Islington, and later that year, on the 26th of September, the trains of East & West India Docks & Birmingham Junction Railway began operating every fifteen minutes into Fenchurch Street. On their journey they skirted the newly opened Victoria Park, and they eventually joined the Blackwall Extension Railway by means of a junction near Bow Common. The first two intermediate stations to be opened along this route were situated at Hackney and Bow, but these were joined by an additional one at Kingsland, just over a month later, on the 9th of November. With the advent of this service, the Blackwall Company felt justified in withdrawing its own trains north-east of Stepney, and both Bow & Bromley, and the branch platforms at Victoria Park & Bow were closed after the last departure on the 25th of September 1850. Although the latter station ceased to serve its intended function after the curtailment of the Fenchurch Street services, it continued to be used by Eastern Counties trains until the 6th of January 1851, after which it was completely closed.

Before the new line was extended westward from Islington to a junction with the parental London & North Western Railway at Chalk Farm, its motive power was supplied by the Blackwall Company, and to help cope with the additional traffic, another locomotive was ordered from Jones & Potts. This was delivered in 1850, and was of the same basic design as before. It became engine No. 7, and it received the name 'Victoria'.

Although the E. & W. I. D. & B. J. R. had to borrow its locomotives for a while, it did in fact possess its own paltry carriages, which according to one contemporary source, had bodies which were made of papier machē. Nevertheless, despite all this apparent poverty, the Company's services proved to be very popular, and during their first month of operation they carried a total of 97,000 passengers.

The new railway was extended to Camden Town on the 7th of December 1850, having been delayed slightly by the collapse of a section of viaduct near Maiden Lane, and on the 15th of November 1851, the Illustrated London News contained the following excellent description of a journey from Fenchurch Street out to the northern suburbs:-

"The trains start every quarter of an hour from half-past eight in the morning till ten at night. There was no puffing or snorting

of the engine, but by a silent signal the train was set in motion. We proceeded for a considerable distance under a covered way, lit by sash windows: this was considered necessary at the original construction of the Blackwall Railway to prevent accidents by horses taking fright from the noise and smoke of the engines as they dart over the bridges crossing the streets of London. (...but there were no engines when the line was first opened!...J.E.C.)

Through the windows we had a glimpse of the Tower of London; but soon emerged from the covered way amid roofs of houses, an ocean of pantiles, and groves of chimneys. We passed the sugar-baking district of Goodman's-fields, the London Docks, Wapping, St George's-in-the-East - a neighbourhood densely populated with a dingy, working or sea-going population. On the left we passed new Shadwell Church, and also St. Mary's Church and Schools, recently erected. We next arrived at Stepney Station and began to breathe more freely, for we had left behind the region of smoke and gigantic chimneys. On the right is the new district church of the parish of Shadwell, built on the site of the house that was so marvellously preserved after the great fire at Ratcliff-cross, which broke out on the 23rd of July, 1794, and which consumed more houses than any one conflagration since the Great Fire of 1666.

On the left, but at some distance from the railway, is seen the square tower of Stepney Church, the mother church of most of the parishes in the eastern part of London. Immediately beneath us on the left is the Commercial-road, leading from Whitechapel to Blackwall, a distance of nearly four miles. Near the junction of the Camden-Town (sic) and Blackwall Railways, Commercial-road is 80 feet in width, and is crossed by an iron viaduct called Bow Spring Bridge, designed by L. Clare Esq., and constructed by Messrs. Fox and Henderson of Birmingham. The reader will perceive that, notwithstanding the great length of the viaduct, and the material of which it is constructed, it has a light and picturesque appearance.

At Stepney Station the Blackwall Railroad forms a junction with the Camden-town Railroad. The former continues its course nearly parallel to the Commercial-road, crossing by a stone bridge the north side of the Regent's Canal Dock, the terminus of the Regent's Canal.

Having crossed the Commercial-road by Bow Spring Bridge, we soon leave the City and Pool of London behind us, and pass through fields to Bow common, where to the right we have an extensive, but distant view of the East India Docks; and beyond them, a view of the Surrey and Kentish hills; on the left, the City of London and Tower Hamlets Cemetery, occupying nearly thirty acres of ground, beautifully disposed, and ornamented with flowers and shrubs. This cemetery with an adjacent field, containing nearly one-hundred and forty acres of land, is about to be purchased by the Commissioners appointed by Act of Parliament to regulate the burial-grounds of the metropolis. Beyond the cemetery is seen the extensive buildings of the City of London Union Workhouse, which from its extent and architecture has a palatial appearance.

We next descended into deep cutting, and passing under the Bow-road, arrived at the Bow Station. Here the train received passengers; and soon after starting we found ourselves in open country: on the right hand the newly-formed Victoria-park; on the left we had an extensive view over the Hackney marshes, terminating with a considerable portion of the well-wooded scenery of Essex.

Passing onward, through the verdant fields we came to the retired village of Homerton, formerly a district of the parish of Hackney, but within the last six years formed into a separate parish; from the railroad is seen a new church, erected about four years ago from the design of Mr. Ashpitel.

The church will accommodate 1,800 persons, and cost less than £5,000, the whole raised by subscriptions. The parsonage house is a pleasing example of domestic architecture. We have now arrived at the Hackney Station: on the right, from the midst of roofs of houses and the thickly-planted trees in the churchyard and adjacent gardens, rises the picturesque tower of the old church; and to the right, the pyramidal tower of the new church. Looking leftward, we were somewhat puzzled at the appearance of several long ditches, or rather trenches, filling with running water, nearly covered with what we took to be weeds; but upon inquiry, we found that this was one of the artificial streams for the continual growth of watercress for the London market. Annexed is a representation of this singular species of cultivation, which affords a living to a great number of poor men, women, and children. The square building on the right hand side is Hackney Railway Station; here the train halted for a few seconds, and then moved on to the Kingsland-road. ..."

From here, the writer described the remainder of the journey, which although extremely interesting, falls well and truly beyond the bounds of this book. It's interesting to note however, that he makes no reference whatsoever to there being a station situated at Shadwell. This is presumably because the trains which worked the service out to North London didn't begin to stop there until the 1st of October 1866, and as the buildings must have been fairly insignificant at that time, he failed to notice them as he passed through.

In the October of 1851, the E. & W. I. D. & B. J. R. opened a new line from Bow, which headed southwards to Poplar, and thence west to a junction with the Blackwall system near West India Docks. At first, this was for the use of coal trains only, but from the 1st of January 1852, general merchandise began to be carried as well. Later in 1852, another connection between the two railways was constructed at Poplar, but this time it projected eastward, and afforded access to Blackwall itself. In common with the western spur, this section was intended for freight purposes only, although as it turned out, the line facing east was later utilised as part of a fairly shortlived passenger route.

With Fenchurch Street in constant use by both L. B. R. and E. & W. I. D. & B. J. R. services, the little two platformed terminus was being stretched to its maximum capacity. Despite this, on the 24th of November 1851, a special meeting of the Blackwall shareholders decided to apply for Parliamentary Authority to build a new line, jointly with the Eastern Counties, from Ilford to Tilbury and Southend. By this time, the ill-feeling which had existed between the two companies had started to recede, and both of them began to realise that co-operation would be more profitable than antagonism. The main idea behind this latest venture was to regain some of the Gravesend traffic which the Blackwall Company was losing as a result of the opening of the direct South Eastern Railway route in 1849.

The new line, which was referred to as 'The London, Tilbury & Southend Extension Railway' was authorised by an Act of Parliament dated the 17th of June 1852, and was built from a junction east of Forest Gate on the Eastern Counties system, through to Barking, Tilbury, Leigh-on-Sea and Southend. At Tilbury, the tracks were laid as a triangle to allow both through running, and also provide access to a small terminus called 'Tilbury Fort'. From here, the L.T. & S.E.R. was to operate its own ferry services across the river, and hopefully benefit from the continuing popularity of Rosherville Gardens.

The new company had four directors appointed by the London & Blackwall, and four by the Eastern Counties, and they chose their old favourite George Parker Bidder as the line's engineer. The actual job of construction was carried out by the firm of Messrs. Peto, Brassey & Betts, who were probably the best known railway builders of their time.

It was proposed to run the new service with one train from Fenchurch Street, and another from Shoreditch, and couple the two together when they met at Stratford. This would mean an extra strain on the already busy tracks between Stepney and the City, and therefore an extra line was mooted on the Up side of the existing formation, together with an enlargement of the facilities available at Fenchurch Street.

The job of widening the viaduct to accommodate the additional track was somewhat lengthy, but the rebuilding of the terminus proved to be rather less so, and the first section of the new station was opened to the public on Saturday, the 19th of November 1853.

Compared to its predecessor, the new structure must have seemed immense, and it had an impressive facade which consisted of eleven bays, each with a tall arched window. At pavement level, six small double doorways were provided, and these were protected from the elements by a rather plain looking canopy which stretched the entire length of the frontage. Adjacent to the north end of the main building was situated a smaller block, which rose to a height of three storeys, and contained the Company's Board Room and General Offices. The top of the main building itself, took the shape of a massive but gracefully curved pediment, which was built to follow the contour of the station's crescent-truss roof, and the whole edifice was constructed of yellow stock bricks.

Inside, at ground level, there were two booking offices; one for the existing services, and the other for the new London, Tilbury & Southend line. From these, two stairways were positioned at either end, which gave access to a small circulating area at the head of the platforms. To help cope with the expected number of travellers, an additional stairway was included at the north end of the frontage, which provided passengers with a direct exit to the street, without having to push their way through the crowded booking hall.

At track level there were four platform faces, sheltered beneath a 300 ft long glass and iron overall roof, which had a total span of 101 ft. The concourse measured the entire width of the station, and was built partially over the top of the booking hall. From its north-eastern corner, there was a passageway which led into the adjacent office block, and therefore gave direct access to the Company's Board Room, which had a lofty ornamented ceiling.

Luggage and parcels were taken from the booking hall to track level by hydraulic lifts, and staff rooms were provided along the south retaining wall, adjacent to Platform One.

The general work of rebuilding the station was carried out by the Westminster firm of J. & C. Rigby, under the direction of George Berkeley, the Railway's Civil Engineer, whilst the roof was constructed by C.J. Mare & Co. of Blackwall.

Because of the hefty job of widening the viaduct, the additional Up line west of Stepney wasn't ready for use until 1856, but in the meantime, many new developments were taking place.

Firstly, the East & West India Docks & Birmingham Junction company had the common sense to change its name to the much more appropriate 'North London Railway' on the 1st of January 1853. Shortly after this, the L. N. W. R. began to use this line to bring freight into the City, and constructed a short branch to serve a new goods depot at Haydon Square, on the north side of the Blackwall viaduct near the Minories. In fact, the Royal Assent had been given for this on the 5th of June 1851, but it wasn't until the 12th of March 1853 that the premises were ready for opening.

The London, Tilbury & Southend Railway, by now short of the 'Extension' bit of its former title, was opened from Forest Gate Junction to Tilbury Fort from the 13th of April 1854, with locomotives and stock provided by the Eastern Counties Company. The trains were worked as originally proposed, with the down Fenchurch Street and Shoreditch portions joining at Stratford, and the corresponding up services dividing at the same place. From the 3rd of July 1854, the joint board of directors leased the line to its builders, Peto, Brassey & Betts, for twenty-one years, on the understanding that they financed its operation, and paid a net return of 6% on the share capital of £400,000, plus half of any surplus profit that might materialise. This change of management however, had no effect on the working of the system, and the trains continued to be supplied by the Eastern Counties Railway.

Back in 1852, two additional locomotives were supplied for the Blackwall services by George England & Co., and these were numbered 8 and 9. Their basic design was very similar to the Jones and Potts No. 7 which had been built two years earlier, although these new machines embodied a few fairly minor detail differences. They were respectively named 'Samson' and 'Hercules', and they were acquired for £1,750 each, in part-exchange for the unsuccessful 'Dwarf' and 'Pygmy Giant'. They were joined in 1860 by another couple of George England products, although this time the locos were 2-4-0 goods tanks with 4' coupled wheels, and 3' leading wheels. These became Nos. 10 and 11 on the Company's books, but as they were intended for hauling merchandise only, they never received any names. They were fitted with two 15" x 22" outside cylinders, and despite the fact that they had a somewhat accentuated overhang at either end, their overall appearance was sturdy and attractive. They were both usefully employed on the system for a little over two decades, but they were eventually replaced by more powerful engines in 1882.

Once the London, Tilbury & Southend Railway became fully operational, it became apparent that the route via Forest Gate was becoming inconvenient, due mainly to the increased number of trains passing over the junction, both on the branch, and also on the Eastern

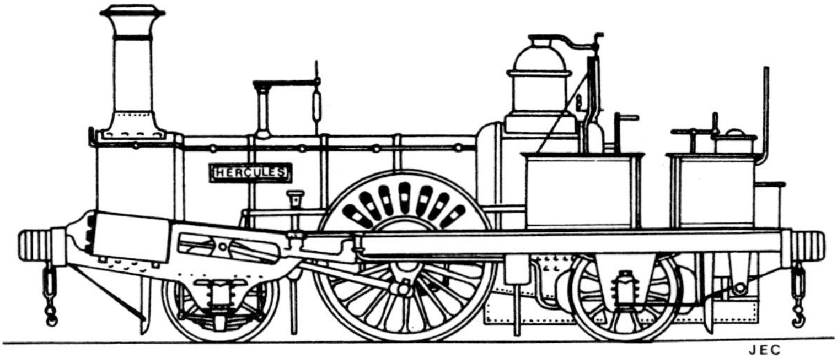

Locomotive No. 9 as originally built in 1852.

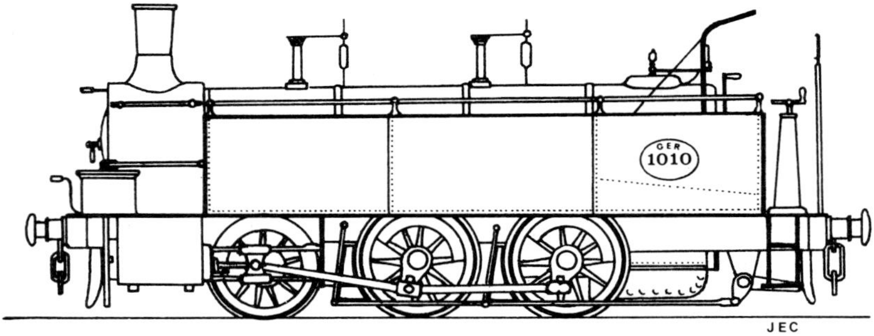

One of the 2-4-0T goods engines as running in later years.

Counties main line to Colchester. The L.T.& S.R. therefore decided to build a new line between Barking and Bow, to give their trains a more direct route into Fenchurch Street. This was authorised by an Act of the 7th of July 1856, and entailed a junction with the Blackwall Extension Railway, slightly north-east of the one already used by the North London services. The signal box which was installed to control this section became known as Gas Factory Junction, and for many years it was staffed by employees of the North London Railway, despite the fact that it was actually the property of the Blackwall Company.

A spur was constructed at Abbey Mills on the new L.T.& S.R. direct line to give trains from the Eastern Counties' North Woolwich branch a better route into Fenchurch Street. The connection was opened on the 1st of June 1858, and from this date, a large proportion of the entire North Woolwich service was diverted from its previous terminus at Shoreditch, and re-routed into Fenchurch Street. In fact, since the summer of 1854, a number of these trains had used the Blackwall's City terminus, but these were forced to travel via Stratford, and therefore had a somewhat longer journey. With the Abbey Mills Spur fully functional, a comprehensive service became possible, and alternate trains from North Woolwich to Fenchurch Street were diagrammed to use the line, whilst the remainder carried on as before.

Now that the two companies were working reasonably happily with each other, the management of the Eastern Counties decided to make more use of the Blackwall Extension Railway, and in an attempt to relieve congestion at its own rather restricted London terminus, it began to operate the majority of its suburban services into Fenchurch Street. With all this new activity, the little railway which started life as an engineering curiosity began to grow up, and soon became an integral part of the contemporary London railway scene.

In fact, more and more use was now being made of the tracks west of Stepney, not only for passenger purposes, but for freight as well. The old Minories station was permanently closed on the 24th of October 1853, and after standing disused for a few years, it was eventually rebuilt as a goods depot. A few historians in the past have expressed a belief that the original passenger buildings were retained for this new function, but judging from the architectural style of the depot, this seems rather unlikely. It was opened on the 1st of August 1858, and for a month or so, it carried the same name as the former station. This was soon altered to 'Mint Street' however, and much later, around 1870, the depot was finally renamed 'Royal Mint Street'. It originally only handled merchandise carried by the L. B. R., E. C. R. and L. T. S. R., but from the 8th of December

1858, it also began to cater for the needs of the Great Northern Railway. To convey wagons from the viaduct to ground level, a hoist was installed, and this was accommodated in the space formerly occupied by the old stationary winding engines.

In 1859, a branch was opened to serve the East India Docks, and following this, the Blackwall directors recommended the construction of another Minories goods depot. This was to be built on the north side of the viaduct, and would be almost opposite the existing one. By now the amount of Great Northern freight traffic had increased to such an extent, that they were offered the exclusive use of the Mint Street premises, and the new establishment was intended to serve the requirements of the L. B. R., E. C. R., and L. T. & S. R.

The new depot took about a year to build, and it was opened for traffic on the 1st of February 1861. Although like its neighbour, it was originally known as 'The Minories', it was soon renamed, and for the rest of its existence it was always known as 'Goodmans Yard'.

Yet another outside company entered the scene in 1862, when the Midland Railway opened their red-brick 'City Goods Station' virtually next door to the G. N. R. Mint Street depot. This became the fourth new installation of its kind to be opened in the vicinity of Fenchurch Street since 1853, so by this time, the line must have been very busy indeed with miscellaneous freight activities.

To promote a better co-ordination between the various railway services in the counties east of London, an Act received the Royal Assent on the 7th of August 1862, which brought about the amalgamation of several companies. The only one of these which had any connection with the Blackwall system was the Eastern Counties, as all the others were provincial concerns which served the townships and backwaters of rural East Anglia. In anticipation of this Act, the new order had taken effect a little over a month earlier, and from that time onwards the combined companies became known as the Great Eastern Railway.

On the 17th of June 1864, this new organisation, with a degree of financial assistance from the London & St. Katherines' Dock Company, opened a short branch on the south side of the Blackwall viaduct, to a goods depot which they called East Smithfield. The tracks which served it, diverged from the main line at London Docks Junction, which was situated a little to the west of the bridge which carried the railway over Leman Street. The line had originally been sanctioned as far back as 1847, at the time when the Blackwall directors were still considering the possible changeover from rope to locomotive haulage, but money was short, and with the general upheaval then besetting the Company, the project remained dormant. The main purpose of the branch was to serve the St. Katherine's

Dock, but although the Parliamentary powers which authorised its construction were renewed in 1851, they again were allowed to lapse due to lack of finances. Eventually a new Act was passed in 1860, but it took a further three years before anybody could afford to have it built. As it was, it fell to the Great Eastern to make the necessary investment, as the Blackwall Company continued to plead poverty. In the end, the Dock Company made an offer to the Railway which guaranteed them 5% on the capital, and this hastened the line's completion. After all this, it seems a crying shame that the scheme was almost a total flop. When it first opened, the branch terminated at a depot on the north side of Upper East Smithfield, but this was changed when the tracks were extended across the road into the dock premises on the 1st of September 1865. Rather than serve the entire dock however, the line came to a feeble halt at the Wool Warehouse, and no further construction was carried out. Despite the aspirations of all concerned, this little extension remained lightly used, and the majority of the traffic continued to be handled at the main depot building. All this aside, from the time that the tracks were fed into the Wool Warehouse, the depot's official title became expanded to 'East Smithfield, London Docks'.

Since the introduction of locomotive haulage back in 1849, there had been few accidents on the Blackwall system which resulted in the loss of human life, and possibly the only serious incident occurred at the Minories in July 1853: A North London train which was passing through the station, left the rails, and squashed two unfortunate platelayers to death against the parapet wall. Surprisingly none of the passengers were seriously injured, although the coaches were reported to have been badly damaged. Another major derailment took place in August 1860, but this time there were no fatalities whatsoever: One of the Blackwall Company's own locomotives jumped the points at Haydon Square Junction, taking its entire train with it. Despite the fact that most of the coaches were overturned, the only casualties managed to escape with a few cuts and bruises.

Apart from odd incidents such as this, the record of the London & Blackwall Railway in its days of independence was one of safety and enterprise. Since 1849, the company had increased its own services, and hosted a number of others, and the spirit of detente which had grown between them and the Eastern Counties led to the two organisations becoming very reliant upon each other. Therefore, it came as no surprise, when a Parliamentary Act was passed in 1865, which leased the little company to the Great Eastern Railway for 999 years. All the shareholders were promised a guaranteed dividend of 4½% on their ordinary capital, and the directors reluctantly relinquished their opulent Board Room at Fenchurch

Street, having first agreed for it to be converted into a First Class Ladies' Waiting Room.

All that the Blackwall financiers now had to do, was sit back and let the money roll in. After all, their worries were over. If the Great Eastern wanted the responsibility, then fair enough they could have it! There was a new managing body now in control of the system, and it was up to them to steer the line's fortunes towards the Twentieth Century.

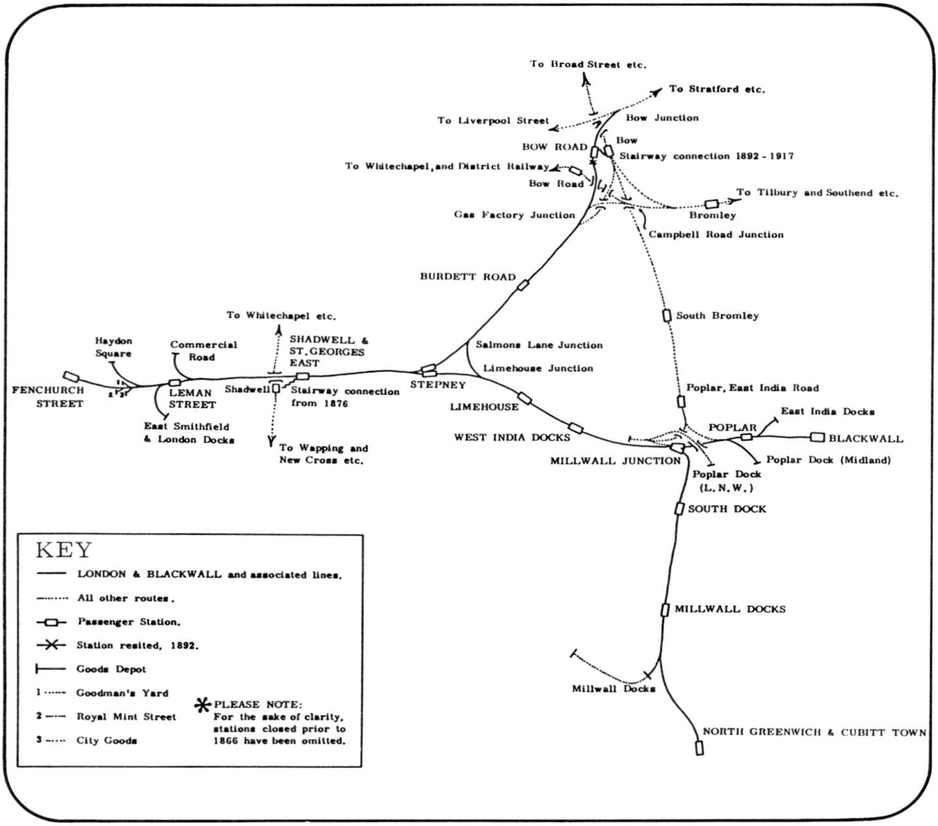

THE LONDON & BLACKWALL SYSTEM 1866-1923.

CHANGING FORTUNES

By the end of the 1850's, the North London Railway found its traffic increasing at such a rate, that a City terminus of its own was becoming an essential. Powers were therefore obtained in 1861 for the construction of an extension which diverged from their line near Kingsland, and terminated at an impressive new station opposite Broad Street. This appendage was referred to at the time as 'The Happy Afterthought', and it was brought into use from the 1st of November 1865.

Initially a through service to Fenchurch Street was provided, which linked the two City termini, but this proved to be very short lived. It was withdrawn after the 1st of August 1866, when the trains from Broad Street were diverted south of Bow, to serve their own route to Poplar, which had previously only been used for freight traffic. This meant that the North London ceased to have any use for their former host, although they continued to operate a connecting service between Bow and Fenchurch Street until the 1st of January 1869, when the responsibility for its operation was passed to the Great Eastern.

This was not the end of the association between the two companies however, as from the 1st of September 1870, the North London extended a number of their Poplar trains into Blackwall. This allowed connections to be made with the steamer services from Brunswick Wharf, and entailed the use of an existing link between the two railways. The short section of line involved had originally been built in 1852 for freight traffic, but once the decision had been made to incorporate it as part of a passenger route, the companies found themselves obliged to have it relaid to a much higher standard.

From the time of their introduction, these trains ran non-stop after leaving the North London Line, and therefore never used the Blackwall Company's station at Poplar. The reason for this was that their own premises were situated only a short distance away, with platforms on the south side of East India Dock Road, and it was deemed unnecessary for them to serve both.

Also around 1870, the Great Northern Railway constructed a goods depot on the north side of the existing branch to East India Dock. This line had originally opened for freight traffic in 1859, and diverged at Brunswick Junction, which was a little to the east of Poplar Station.

The new Great Northern establishment was at first intended for shipping traffic only, but after serving this function for about thirty years, it began to handle general merchandise as well.

With all this going on, the line was becoming well integrated into the expanding network of London's railways, but perhaps the most important development during this period was the opening of a short branch to serve the Isle of Dogs.

This had originally been suggested by the Blackwall directors back in the summer of 1863, but their Bill was refused the necessary Parliamentary Authority. Until this time, the area through which they intended the line should run consisted largely of desolate swamps, and indeed the entire district had once been known by the name of 'Stepney Marsh'. Things began to change however, with the development of the docks, and the Company's intention was to get their branch built before the price of land rose any higher. With this in mind, they again applied for permission to proceed, and this time their application fortunately met with a better response. On the 19th of June 1865, an Act was passed which sanctioned its construction, and the scheme which was known as 'The London, Blackwall & Millwall Extension Railway' at last became a reality.

The branch was designed to leave the main line at a junction near Harrow Lane, Poplar, then run southwards to a riverside terminus in Johnson Street, which was about 200 yards from the jetty used by the Greenwich ferries. These had a long history, which in fact dated back to 1550, when King Edward VI originally authorised Sir Thomas Wentworth to operate them. From 1676 onwards the boats had been provided by a company which was known as 'The Potters Ferry Society', although much later, these were joined by others which worked a statutory service for horses and vehicles, created by the passing of the Poplar and Greenwich Ferry Act in 1812. Apart from serving trade and industry around Millwall, one of the principal aims of this new line was to link Fenchurch Street with these ferries, and the name allotted to the branch terminus was 'North Greenwich'.

The line was jointly promoted by the Blackwall Railway and the Millwall Canal Company, the latter of which was then actively engaged in the completion of their new Millwall Docks. It was to have a total length of 1 mile, 49 chains, and have two intermediate stations.

The Millwall Canal Company were perhaps fortunate in having a General Manager whose opposite number on the Great Eastern happened to be his brother, and therefore the two organisations were on the best of terms with each other. However, the same thing couldn't be said of the relationship between the Railway and the East & West India Docks Company, who saw the line as a threat to their livelihood. During the planning stages they made numerous technical objections about its construction, but basically their main complaint was that its existence would give the rival Millwall Company a right of way over their property. Eventually however, after much arguing and the intervention of an arbitrator, the opposition was dropped from the 21st of March 1865, when the bodies concerned finally reached an agreement regarding the line's operation. This meant that sections of the track which passed through the Dock Companies' premises, would in fact be owned by the relevant authorities, and the trains which travelled along them would have to be hauled by horses to avoid any risk of fire.

The process of sorting out the various objections hindered the construction of the line, and by the end of 1867, only a short section between the junction and the south side of the West India Docks was ready for use. The following year, the period allowed for its completion was extended by Parliament until 1871, which was just as well, as the miniscule part which linked the West India and Millwall Docks actually took an amazing four years to build! By the time that it opened on the 18th of December 1871, the Millwall Dock had been fully functional for over three years, and its owners had changed their title to the more appropriate 'Millwall Dock Company'.

At first trains only operated as far as the station at Millwall Docks, but from the 29th of July 1872, these were extended to North Greenwich.

Because of the various level crossings and frail timber bridges, the line was basically a light railway, and for a while at least, the use of locomotives had to be ruled out. Despite its diminutive length, it was managed by no less than three organisations, each of whom were responsible for their own section of line.

The first five chains were retained by the Railway, followed by 41 chains which were owned by the East & West India Docks, and 52 chains belonging to the Millwall Docks. The final 31 chains were again London & Blackwall property, and consisted largely of a 682 yard brick viaduct, which crossed Manchester Road and Wharf Road a little short of the terminus in Johnson Street.

The branch started from a new station between West India Docks and Poplar, which received the name of Millwall Junction. Although this was technically correct, in so much as this was the place where passengers were required to change trains if they wished to travel to Millwall, it was nevertheless rather misleading, as it wasn't actually situated on the Isle of Dogs itself. It was reached by a footbridge which led onto the premises from the south end of Harrow Lane, and a booking office was provided at track level. The main building which stood on the platform between the up main and diverging branch, was at first fairly inadequate, but this was replaced by a more substantial red brick structure when the station was rebuilt in 1888. There were three platform faces in all, with two on the Blackwall side, and one for the North Greenwich trains. The branch platform curved sharply to the south-east, and here passengers could join a single tram-like vehicle which was hauled by two horses along the single line to Millwall Docks.

From Millwall Junction, the branch made a sharp ascent, and then crossed the entrances to the West India Import and Export Docks, before reaching the isolated little station called South Dock. This was surrounded by timber yards, and was some distance from the nearest main road, and yet it was equipped with the line's only passing loop, and also housed the head office of the managing committee. The structure itself was largely built of wood, although it was fitted with a slate roof, and also stood on a solid, brick-faced platform. Being totally within the estate of the East & West India Company, it was entirely staffed by dock employees, and it also issued tickets which carried its owner's initials or name.

The same rule applied to the tickets from the next station, although here the two booking clerks and two porters were all employed by the Railway. It was built on the south side of Glengall Road, near the junction with East Ferry Road, and it carried the name of Millwall Docks. As before, the buildings were largely wooden, as indeed was the platform, but unlike South Dock it never had a passing loop. Some contemporary documents show its full name as 'Millwall Docks (Glengall Road)', but this suffix never appeared on the station nameboards nor on the tickets that were issued there. The actual structure was situated on an embankment, and trains leaving the previous station had to cross a large swing bridge, which spanned the entrance to the South Dock itself, and then pass through the boundary gate of the Millwall Dock Company. So intense was the rivalry between these two organisations, that this gate would always be locked across the rails after the passage of the last evening train and not reopened again until they started running the following morning. Once beyond here, the trains would skirt the east side of the Dock, and then start the stiff climb towards Glengall Road. Being clear of the worst potential fire hazards, the boundary gate of the Millwall Dock Company was where the horses were taken off, and replaced for the remainder of the journey by a steam locomotive.

The first of these to be employed was a strange antiquated machine named 'Ariels Girdle', which had been built in 1851 as Works No. 270, by Messrs. Kitson, Thompson & Hewitson at their Airedale Foundry in Leeds. It was originally constructed as a 2-2-0 well tank, and whilst it was still brand new it was displayed at the Great Exhibition in Hyde Park. After this, it was sold to the Eastern Union Railway, who numbered it 28, but when its new owners were absorbed by the Eastern Counties system three years later, it was renumbered 17. It continued in its original form for another fifteen years, until its performance whilst fitted with a single pair of 5' driving wheels began to prove unsatisfactory. Because of this, it was taken into Stratford Works for conversion into a 2-4-0T, and the rebuilt engine emerged in 1868, sporting new 4' drivers and a replacement pair of 9" x 15" cylinders.

About the same time as this was sent to work the Millwall services, it was placed on the Great Eastern's duplicate list, and therefore was given the new number of 17A. It was also equipped with a spark arrester to minimise the risk of lineside fires, and the loco later became known to the people of Cubitt Town as the 'I Can Do It'.

It remained on the branch until about 1875, when its place was taken by one of the old Jones & Potts 2-2-2 well tanks from the Blackwall main line. This was No. 97, which prior to being taken over by the Great Eastern had been numbered 6, and had carried the name 'Thames' This loco worked the trains until 1880, although it sometimes shared its duties with an obscure vertical boilered tram engine which had been built by Kitsons.

Because the locomotives were not allowed to pass through the West India Dock premises 'in steam', they had to be towed by horses when they were taken away for servicing, and this meant that their fires had to be 'drawn' at the southern end, then re-lit for the remainder of their journey at Millwall Junction.

The section of track on which they operated included the long arched viaduct which commenced a few yards south of Millwall Docks station, and continued uninterrupted as far as Manchester Road, where an iron bridge carried the tracks onto a much shorter brick section, which led to the terminus itself.

The area which this was to serve was then being developed as a new working class residential district known as 'Cubitt Town', but as the Great Eastern wanted a more 'up-market' image for their station, they decided to give it the title of 'North Greenwich'. Nevertheless, the name 'Cubitt Town' was generally shown as a suffix on tickets and other printed matter, and therefore it was not omitted altogether.

The main building stood on the east side of Johnson Street (now Ferry Street), and although this was largely wooden, it had a frontage which was built of brick. This facade was totally devoid of architectural embellishment, and comprised an access doorway at either end, and four small sash windows on the first floor. At track

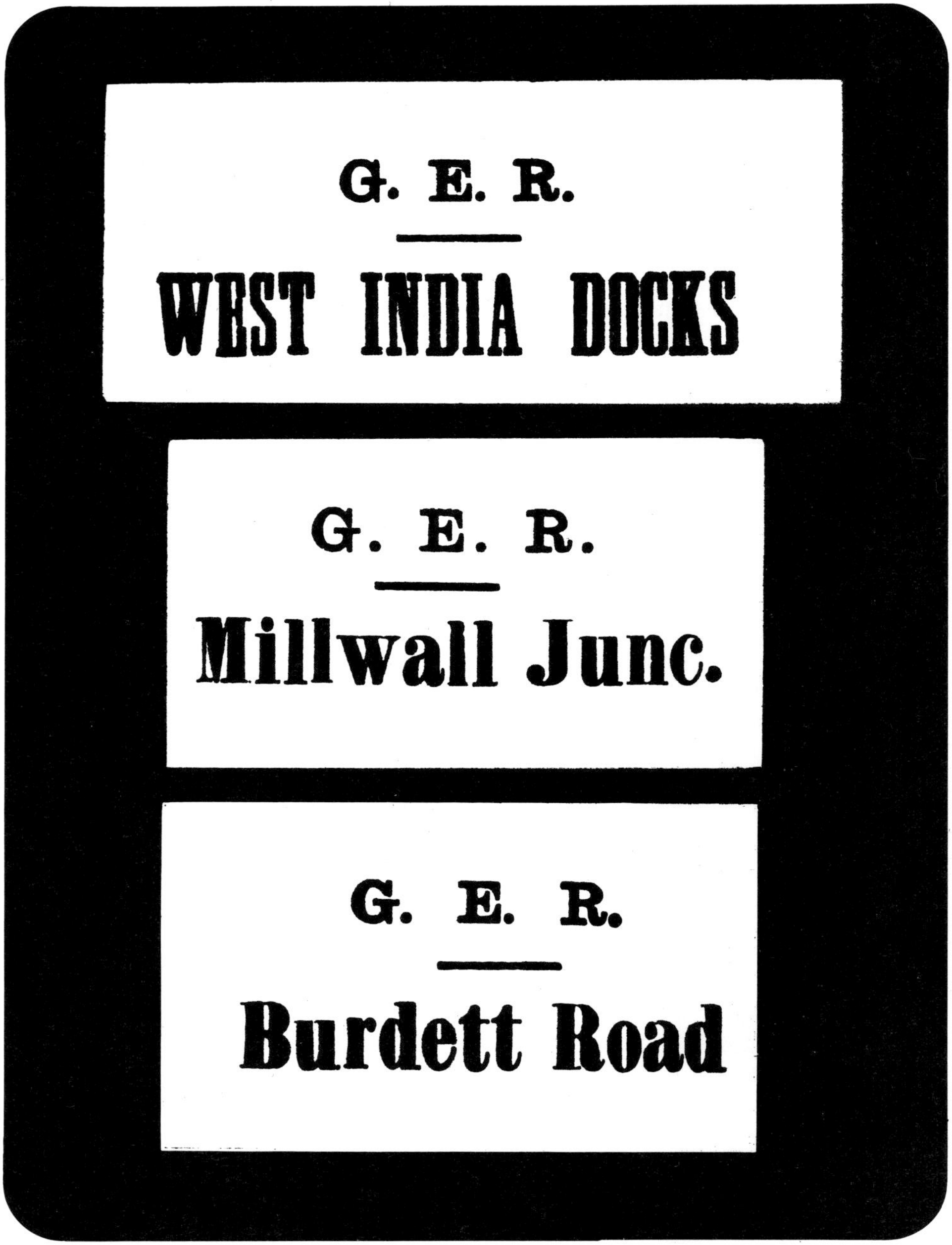

A SELECTION OF G.E.R. LUGGAGE LABELS

level, both buildings and platforms were constructed of wood, and a canopy was provided which had valancing of a very plain and simple type. The rails finished at a set of buffer stops behind a protective wall overlooking the river, and although there were storage sidings for carriages, there were no facilities to cater for freight traffic. A small engine-shed was erected on the east side of the line, and a water tower and run-round facilities were also installed.

As far as the trains were concerned, the initial passenger service was provided largely for dock employees, and was worked at half-hourly intervals between 8.30 am and 4.30 pm. This was altered to a starting time of 7.30 am, and had its frequency increased to four every hour, when the opening of North Greenwich was becoming imminent in the June of 1872. Although the branch was functioning throughout from the 29th of July, it seems that it remained unadvertised until the following November, when it first appeared in a public timetable. Nevertheless, since the first section opened, the line had been used by goods trains although as there were no freight facilities at the terminus, none of these ever ventured further south than a small depot which was situated a short distance beyond Millwall Docks.

With the Millwall Extension Railway virtually completed, the Company turned their attentions to other parts of the system, and the 1870's saw the construction of three new stations.

The first of these was sited at Burdett Road, between Stepney and Bow, and opened on Monday the 11th of September 1871. Because of limited space at street level, the station entrance was incorporated within the structure of the viaduct itself, and a pair of internal stairways were fitted which led up from the gloomy booking hall to the two platforms. These stretched along the bridge that crossed the main road, and for most of their length they were covered by a long shallow canopy. This was fitted with a style of valancing which was fairly unusual for the Great Eastern, although a similar design was later used for many stations on the suburban system of the London Brighton & South Coast Railway. The buildings themselves were largely made of wood, but also had brickwork added at the rear to increase their strength.

When Burdett Road first opened, the Great Eastern published a handbill which advertised it as having trains every fifteen minutes to both Fenchurch Street and Bow 'New Station'. The reason for the suffix on the latter was because the North London premises at Bow had recently been totally rebuilt, and what had been a fairly ordinary little station had been transformed into an enormous construction, as proud in its appearance as any main line terminus. The service that linked it with Fenchurch Street had been provided by the Great Eastern since the 1st of January 1869, when it had been relinquished by the North London, and the fares for a single journey were 6d First Class, 4d Second Class and 3d Third Class. The trains operated from 7.45 am to 10.30 pm on weekdays, and 8.15 am to 10.30 pm on Sundays, although the latter had a break for church services between 11.00 am and 1.00pm.

Around the same time as Burdett Road was completed, work was well under way on another station. This was at Leman Street, on a site slightly east of the junction with the London Docks branch. The entrance was situated adjacent to the south side of the viaduct, and wooden stairways were employed to provide access to the platforms. Although it was ready for use in 1872, the Board of Trade regarded the structure as being unsafe, and subsequently refused to sanction its opening. Because of this the entire station had to be completely rebuilt, and therefore it was not brought into commission until the 1st of June 1877.

With the increasing number of trains between Fenchurch Street and Stratford, the Company decided to build a new station on the site of the old Bow & Bromley, and this they gave the more appropriate title of Bow Road. The booking office took the form of a small brick building on the east side of the railway, from which stairs ascended to the wooden platforms. Because of the restricted width available at track level, these had to be cantilevered from the side of the viaduct, and their construction was therefore somewhat flimsy. Nevertheless, this time the Board of Trade made no objection to the quality of the finished product, and the station was opened to the public on the 1st of October 1876.

Earlier that year, the Company undertook the hefty task of renewing the bridge which carried the Blackwall Extension Railway over Commercial Road. This entailed the piece-meal removal of the old iron girders, and the substitution of new ones without unduly interfering with the flow of traffic. The work of reconstruction was supervised by Mr. Langley, who was one of the Railway's engineers, and it was carried out by the firm of Messrs. Handyside & Company of London and Derby. When it was completed in May, the new bridge enabled the road beneath to be widened by about 18 inches, and also prompted improvements to the Bow line platforms at Stepney station. The person responsible for the design of the rebuilt structure was the Contractor's engineer, Mr. Norman Garrard.

Another alteration that was carried out in 1876, was the construction of a stairway interchange with the East London Railway at Shadwell. This enabled London & Blackwall passengers to purchase through tickets to destinations south of the river, and gave them direct access to the line which had recently been opened through

Marc Brunel's Thames Tunnel. The existence of this facility, coupled with an erstwhile unfulfilled scheme to install a physical link between the tracks of the East London and Blackwall Railways, probably inspired a rather unlikely series of loco namings. The engines concerned were the London Brighton and South Coast A1 class 0-6-0 tanks, which in addition to other suburban duties, regularly worked through the Thames Tunnel. These machines were built between 1872 and 1880, and the fact that some of them once spent much of their time beneath the ground, earned them the nickname of 'Terriers'. The locomotives which bore the names of stations on the Blackwall system were numbered 38, 55, 70, 72, 74, 75 and 79, and these were known respectively as 'Millwall', 'Stepney', Poplar', Fenchurch', 'Shadwell', 'Blackwall' and 'Minories'. The majority of these commemorated contemporary places served by the line, but the choice of name for No. 79 seems a bit strange, as the station concerned had been closed for well over twenty years when the loco was built. Many of these engines had a very long working life, and both 'Stepney' and 'Fenchurch' can still be seen on the Bluebell Railway in Sussex.Another of this group, No.70 'Poplar' is preserved on the Kent & East Sussex Railway, although it is currently painted in British Railways black, and no longer carries its name.

Since its opening, Shadwell station had only been used by the trains which journeyed to Blackwall or Bow, but after 1875 these were joined by all the other Fenchurch Street services that were operated by the Great Eastern.

At the southern end of the Millwall Extension Railway, the Company acquired the rights to operate the ferries to Greenwich in 1874. This they did after successful negotiations with the Thames Steamboat Company, who had in fact leased the services from the Potters Ferry Society only three years earlier. To improve the connection between the trains and boats, a new pier was constructed adjacent to the branch terminus in 1877, and this was equipped with a covered way which led directly on to the station platform. After this was completed, through bookings were introduced which included the price of the crossing, and these tickets always referred to the landing stage across the river as 'South Greenwich'. The cost of a return from Fenchurch Street was 1/2d First Class, 11d Second Class and 8d Third Class, and the inclusive journey time from the City was around 36 minutes.

After much deliberation, the insurance companies responsible for the interests of the East and West India Docks finally agreed that the North Greenwich branch could be operated throughout by steam locomotives, and in anticipation of this decision, the Joint Committee placed an order for three small 2-4-0 tank engines with the well known Leeds firm of Manning Wardle. The Railway took delivery of two of these in the March of 1880, but the construction of the third loco was delayed somewhat, and it wasn't completed until the following November.

The Board of Trade Inspector, Colonel Yolland, officially sanctioned the change-over after he visited the line on the 4th of August 1880, and following this, on the 21st of the same month, the horses which previously worked the branch returned to their stables at Millwall Junction for the last time. As this was prior to the introduction of a Sunday service, the initial two engines didn't enter traffic until Monday the 23rd, but once they started operating, the timetable was amended, and the trains began to work a seven-day week.

Whereas 'Ariels Girdle' and the Kitson tram engine could perhaps best be described as 'curiosities', the outward appearance of these little 2-4-0Ts was an absolute delight. To conform to the various restrictions imposed on the branch, they were built to very light specifications, and had four tiny 3'6" driving wheels, and two inside 9" x 18" cylinders. They were originally painted dark yellow, in a style which was reminiscent of the one then used by the London Brighton & South Coast Railway, but this was later changed to a shade of brick red, lined out in black. Their domes, number plates and chimney caps were made of burnished brass, and the footplate crews took a great pride in keeping their engines clean.

Even though the locomotives only weighed a little over 16 tons, the bridges on the branch had to be strengthened before they entered traffic, but once they did, the Railway's Joint Committee were able to introduce a more frequent service of trains. These operated every weekday at fifteen minute intervals between 7 am and 6 pm, and every thirty minutes after that until 10 o'clock. The Sunday workings were half-hourly throughout the day between 7.45 am and 10 pm, but these had a break between 11 am and 1 pm in accordance with the wishes of those who attended church. The station at South Dock, which was mainly used by workmen, closed after half-past six on weekday evenings, and never opened at all on Sundays. All of the trains on the North Greenwich branch connected with those on the main line, although there was never a through service from Fenchurch Street.

The locomotives, which were nick-named 'Coffee-Pots', were officially the property of the Joint Committee responsible for the line's operation, and were never regarded as part of the Great Eastern's stock. They were numbered 3, 4 and 6, although these were changed to 28, 29 and 31, when the engines were taken over by the P. L. A. in 1909. When they were first introduced, they were fitted with handbrakes only, but these were supplemented with

Westinghouse equipment around 1892. To cut down on the risk of line-side fires, the locos were furnished with spark-arresters, which were first placed on the tops of their chimneys, but later modified and fitted internally. For a number of years the engines ran with advertisements for Pear's Soap painted on their tank sides, with the name and address of Walter Hill's, the agency responsible, printed on the sandboxes for good measure. By 1905, they were in dire need of rejuvenation, and the three of them were sent to East Ferry Road Engineering Company for rebuilding. When they emerged, they had new $9\frac{1}{2}$" x 16" cylinders, and in this form they continued in service for a number of years.

The original numbering system placed the little Manning Wardles in the same series as the locomotives which were independently owned by the Millwall Dock Company. This was the first organisation of its kind in London to have its own internal railway system, and its engines were used largely for shunting around the quaysides and yards. They were all small saddle tanks, and they carried the numbers 1, 2, 5 and 7. Of these, No. 2 is known to have deputised on the passenger service, and on several occasions it appeared at the head of a rake of coaches when a 2-4-0T was not available. This particular engine was an inside cylinder 0-6-0ST which was built by Hunslets of Leeds in 1880, and carried the name 'Bee'. The other locos presumably also worked on the branch, but the majority of their lives appear to have been spent within their Company's boundary, and they are believed to have been confined only to very local freight traffic. Apart from these machines however, other visitors to the line included standard Great Eastern goods engines, which were often employed on ballast workings, but because these trains were so heavy, they had to be restricted to 4 mph whilst they were crossing the swing bridges.

The rolling stock used on the branch comprised of 8 oil-lit coaches which were hired from the Great Eastern. Three of these were 1st/2nd composites, two were ordinary 3rds, and the remainder were brake 3rds. Normally the trains were formed of three coaches, but this was generally reduced to two at the slack period around mid-day. The line was usually worked with two engines in steam, and the other one kept as a spare at North Greenwich. In true Joint Committee spirit, the locomotive crews were employed by the dock companies, whilst the guards were members of the Great Eastern's staff.

Between Millwall Junction and the terminus, there were three level crossings, and six signal boxes, only the one at North Greenwich was staffed by the railway company, as the rest were manned by dock workers. The line was worked on the Tyer's lock and block system, and was single for its entire length, except for the passing loop at South Dock. There were also various extended sidings which served the needs of the freight trains which operated to and from the docks, but these were never used for passenger purposes.

A regular early morning service for dockland employees was introduced in July 1883, although a Penny Workman's Train had in fact operated since 1872. Apart from these the line was generally lightly used, although for a while it became very busy on Saturdays with additional football traffic. This started in 1885, when the team then known as Millwall Rovers began playing on a piece of waste land in Glengall Road. When this was required for a dock extension in 1901, the Club were obliged to move to a ground nearer to North Greenwich. On days when they were playing 'At Home', the trains from Millwall Junction had to be strengthened to five coaches, which when full, must have taxed the little engines to their limits. This happy state of affairs for the finances of the line ceased in 1910 however, when the Millwall Football Club moved their headquarters to New Cross, although by this time the fortunes of the branch were in decline anyway.

Six years after the North Greenwich line was opened, the Great Eastern was prompted by an increasing number of public complaints to ask the London & Blackwall directors to finance a series of station improvements. Amongst these were modifications which they felt were necessary at Fenchurch Street, as by this time the little terminus was again feeling the strain of overcrowding. To this effect an Act had been passed by Parliament in 1876, which not only authorised the alterations at the City end, but also called for the rebuilding of the majority of the earlier intermediate stations. Most of the work at Fenchurch Street entailed the rearrangement of the track layout, and when this was completed in 1883, the remodelled terminus had been equipped with five platform faces. Of these, Number One was sited alongside the south wall, and was used exclusively for the Blackwall services. This was the shortest of them all and measured only a mere 380 ft. Next to this was a 555 ft island which carried the numbers Two and Three. These were used largely by the Great Eastern suburban trains to Ilford and Ongar, and were protected by canopies where they protruded beyond the limits of the overall roof. After this was positioned an engine road, followed by the station's longest platform, the 765 ft Number Four. This was used by the L.T. & S.R., whose status as a totally independent Company had just been confirmed by an Act of the 24th of July 1882. The remaining face was Number Five, and this took the form of a bay at the east end of Number Four. This had a length of 470 ft., and was used by the services to North Woolwich, and slightly later, to the Royal Albert Dock. Sometimes the Woolwich trains used

Number Three on Sundays, as indeed did the occasional working from the L. T. & S. R., but normally these services kept to their usual allotted platforms. Around 1881, a five-storeyed office block was erected in John Street to cater for the administrative needs of the Blackwall organisation and the L. T. & S. R., and on its ground floor was positioned an additional station entrance, which was linked by stairs to platforms Four and Five.

Apart from the work at Fenchurch Street, the stations at Shadwell, Stepney, Limehouse, West India Docks and Poplar also received a fair amount of treatment, although this was confined largely to the renewal of structures, and therefore required less drastic alterations than those at the terminus. At Limehouse however, a new line was constructed, which started a little to the west of the platforms, and joined the Blackwall Extension line between Stepney and Burdett Road stations. This became known as the 'Limehouse Curve', and it was opened for freight traffic on the 5th of April 1880. It consisted mainly of brick viaduct, although the bridges which crossed Commercial Road and Salmon Lane were both of iron. Its construction had been authorised by an Act of Parliament dated 1877, and it took just over a year to complete.

At the beginning of 1880, the Great Eastern, intent on making money from the pleasure traffic to Alexandra Palace, started to provide a passenger service between Fenchurch Street and Palace Gates, but from the 1st of September, this was diverted by way of the new line, and began to operate from Blackwall. Unfortunately however, the hoped-for profits never materialised, and after just a few months of working, the trains were withdrawn from the 1st of March 1881. A few through excursions from Blackwall to Southend used the line during the summers of 1890 and 1891, but even these were not particularly successful, and therefore the Company finally gave up the idea of using it for anything other than freight purposes.

In 1880, there appeared the first of a long line of 4-4-2 tank locomotives which were built for the L.T. & S.R. These were designed by William Adams, who back in 1868, had produced a series of 4-4-0 passenger tanks for the North London Railway. Because the Company were not able to construct them themselves, the L. T. & S. R. General Manager and Resident Engineer, Mr. Arthur Lewis Stride, placed an order with the Manchester firm of Sharp Stewart for twelve engines at a price of £1,970 each. This contract was authorised on the 24th of July 1879, and their delivery began in the following April. The locos had 6'1" driving wheels, and two outside 17"x 26" cylinders. Their full weight in working order was around 56 tons, and they had a length from buffer to buffer of 36' 9". They were very attractive machines, painted in the new L. T. & S. R.

green livery, lined out in red, white and black. Each one received the name of a station or a district served by their system, and this was carried on their tank sides, painted in a shallow arc above the Company's crest. No. 1 was called 'Southend', No. 2 'Gravesend', and so on down to No. 12 which was named 'Pitsea'. It wasn't until a later batch that any received the titles associated with the Blackwall Line, and by this time the locomotives were being constructed under the supervision of the new Chief Mechanical Engineer, Mr. Thomas Whitelegg. Of these, numbers 29 and 30, which were both built in 1884, received the names of 'Stepney' and 'Fenchurch' respectively; whilst No. 45, of a slightly modified 1898 design came out as 'Burdett Road'. Sometimes the locomotives exchanged names with their sister engines when they went through the paintshops, and in this manner No. 45 appeared as 'Shoeburyness' in 1911, whilst No. 18 which had previously carried that title became 'Burdett Road'. Renamings of this nature no doubt caused a certain amount of confusion at the time, but nevertheless it's nice to relate that the L.T.& S.R. used such delightfully homely names for their engines, rather than delving into the depths of obscure classical mythology for their inspiration as did a few of their contemporaries.

It says a lot for these locomotives that their basic design admittedly with numerous detail differences, was still being used for new engines until 1930, and that some were still running well over a quarter of a century later. Until the first one appeared in 1880, the motive power for the Tilbury and Southend services was still provided by the Great Eastern, although the L. T. & S. R. supplied its own coaching stock from 1877 onwards. One of the 1909 batch of 'Tilbury Tanks', No. 80, 'Thundersley' was painted in a representation of its old livery for the line's Centenary Celebrations in 1956, and is now preserved at the Bressingham Steam Museum in Norfolk.

About the time that the new L. T. & S. R. 4-4-2Ts were making their debut at Fenchurch Street, the Great Eastern were in the process of exterminating the last of the old London & Blackwall 2-2-2 well tanks, which they had inherited in 1866.

During their last fifteen years or so, the whole class had been subject to a number of minor changes, although their basic design remained largely unaltered. Some of them had been fitted with larger domes under the direction of Mr. S. W. Johnson, but apart from this, the most noticeable modification was carried out on the instigation of William Adams, and entailed the replacement of the original bell-mouthed chimneys with new ones of the stove pipe type. This gave the engines a vastly different character, and by updating their image a little, it possibly helped to improve their appearance. Unfortunately however, the same thing cannot be said

Minories Station, looking east in 1840.
The Penny Magazine of the Society for the Diffusion of Useful Knowledge.

Fenchurch Street station concourse around the turn of the century. The entrance to Platform One, used by Blackwall services can be seen to the extreme right of the photograph. *Lens of Sutton.*

Docklands Light Railway Unit No. 04 at Tower Gateway station in September 1987. *J.E.Connor.*

Docklands Light Railway Unit No. 06 passes the site of the old Midland Railway City Goods station in Septmber 1987. *C.D.J.Connor.*

The exterior of Fenchurch Street in January 1984.

J.E.Connor.

Ex-G.E.R. Class J65 0-6-0T No. 156 leaves Leman Street with the 3.30 pm Blackwall to Fenchurch Street train on the 28th of March 1925. *L.C.G.B. Ken Nunn Collection.*

Ex-G.E.R. Class J65 0-6-0T (running as a 2-4-0T) No. 7155 leaves Leman Street with the 1.40 pm Fenchurch Street - Blackwall train on 28th of March 1925. *L.C.G.B. Ken Nunn Collection.*

Ex-G.E.R. Class J65 0-6-0T No. 7249 leaving Leman Street with the 12.05 pm Blackwall to Fenchurch Street train on the 28th of March 1925. *L.C.G.B. Ken Nunn Collection.*

Ex-G.E.R. Class J65 0-6-0T (running as a 2-4-0T) No. 155 stands at Leman Street with a Blackwall to Fenchurch Street train sometime around 1925. *Lens of Sutton.*

The down side of the disused Shadwell & St. Georges East station in 1950. *D.Nelson.*

The remains of Shadwell & St. Georges East station viewed from a train using the 'fast' lines on the north side of the viaduct. The photograph was taken late in 1955, a short while before the structure was demolished. *David Blackwell.*

The new D.L.R. station at Shadwell, seen on the first day of public service with Unit No.11 en-route from Tower Gateway to Island Gardens. *C.D.J.Connor.*

The interior of Stepney East booking hall in 1984. *J.E.Connor.*

Stepney East in the 1930's showing the Bow Line on the left, and the Blackwall branch on the right. The old signal tower dating from the early days of locomotive haulage can be seen immediately left of the signal box. *National Railway Museum.*

The main building on the Up Bow Line platform at Stepney East (now Limehouse) looking west in August 1982. *J.E.Connor.*

The Blackwall Viaduct looking towards the Regents Canal Basin in January 1984. *J.E.Connor.*

The site of the former Blackwall line platforms at Stepney East (now Limehouse) looking west in January 1984. The flat area on the left marks the spot where the up side stairwell once surfaced.
J. E. Connor.

Docklands Light Railway test train from Tower Gateway to Island Gardens arrives at Limehouse early in July 1987. *J. E. Connor*

The Blackwall viaduct, derelict and seemingly without a future in 1981. The view is looking east towards Limehouse Junction.
J.E.Connor.

The trackbed of the Limehouse Curve, looking towards Limehouse Junction in 1984. The hydraulic accumulator tower built for the Regents Canal Dock in 1852 can be seen beyond the bridge.
J.E.Connor.

Docklands Light Railway Unit No. 05 leaves Limehouse and passes the Regents Canal Basin which can be seen on the right. Reproduction L.& B.R. railings have been added along the top of the viaduct.

C.D.J.Connor.

Westferry station, D.L.R. looking east on the 31st of August 1987.

J.E.Connor.

The down platform at the original Limehouse station in 1921. *British Rail*

Millwall Junction station looking east. *National Railway Museum.*

H.M.the Queen, accompanied by Prince Philip, and escorted by Sir Keith Bright, the chairman of London Regional Transport alighting from the 'Royal Train' at Poplar station. Thursday 30th July 1987.
East London Advertiser.

The first D.L.R. public service, the 05.17 Poplar to Island Gardens prepares to set out on its historic journey. 31.8.1987. *J.E.Connor.*

Former Midland Railway Battery Shunter B.E.L. No. 1 awaits breaking up in 1965. *J.E.Connor*

Midland Signal Box at Poplar Dock in 1952.
Bob Stanley/G.H.Ward Collection.

Poplar Junction looking east in the summer of 1965. The Midland Railway's Dock Branch diverged to the right, whilst the main line to Blackwall continued to the left. *J.E.Connor.*

Poplar station looking west, sometime in the 1950's. *Lens of Sutton.*

The exterior of Blackwall station as it appeared in the 1930's.
National Railway Museum.

A platform view of Blackwall, taken after closure.
National Railway Museum.

Ex-G.E.R. J65 Class 0-6-0T (running as a 2-4-0T), No. 158 leaves Blackwall with the 1.35 train to Fenchurch Street on the 25th of July 1925. *L.C.G.B. Ken Nunn Collection.*

A train for North Greenwich stands at Millwall Junction, headed by Manning Wardle 2-4-0T No. 6. *Lens of Sutton.*

Millwall Extension Railway locomotive No. 6 on a North Greenwich train at South Dock. *Lens of Sutton.*

A North Greenwich branch train at Millwall Docks. *Lens of Sutton.*

Millwall Docks station after closure, looking northwards along East Ferry Road towards the junction with Glengall Road. *Lens of Sutton.*

Millwall Extension Railway locomotive No. 4 stands at North Greenwich station with the branch train from Millwall Junction.
L.C.G.B. Ken Nunn Collection.

North Greenwich station looking north: 2-4-0T No. 4 stands at the platform. *L.C.G.B. Ken Nunn Collection.*

The exterior of the former North Greenwich terminus in 1968.
J.E.Connor.

The street level remains of Burdett Road station in 1984, looking north. The actual entrance was situated within the pedestrian archway.
J.E.Connor.

The up side platform at Burdett Road in 1955. A rare picture of a seemingly little photographed station. *David Blackwell.*

The street level building of the 1892 Bow Road station, as it appeared in the spring of 1968. *J.E.Connor.*

Bow Road station looking towards Stratford in 1942. *British Rail.*

Ex-L.N.E.R. N7 0-6-2T No. 69733 heads a train from Ilford to Fenchurch Street at Bow Road in August 1949. *H.C.Casserly.*

Bow Road station in 1948, after the length of its canopies had been reduced. Compare this with the similar view on the previous page which was taken six years earlier. *Lens of Sutton.*

The derelict Up platform at Bow Road in 1966. *J.E.Connor.*

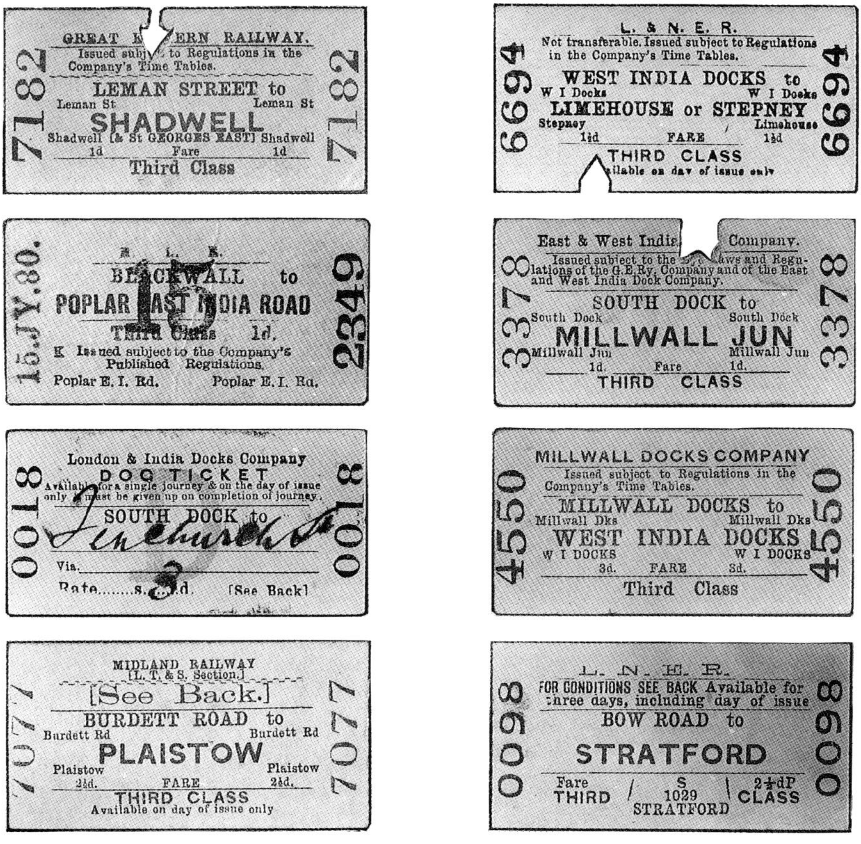

A SMALL SELECTION OF TICKETS. *J.E.Connor and P.D'Arcy.*

of their paintwork, which changed from the distinctive royal blue to an insipid and sickly shade of pea green. For a while the engines were not lined out, and the only relieving features were the large eliptical brass number plates which were fitted on the footplate side-sheets. In fact, it was only after 1866 that these machines were actually furnished with these, as in their independent days the numbers were generally only painted on the buffer-beams. Nevertheless, although the Great Eastern were responsible for this little embellishment, they also regrettably removed their names, and for nearly two decades they continued to run around in this undistinguished manner. One improvement which was carried out however, concerned the buffers, where the old padded leather examples were replaced by those of the sprung metal variety some time around the take-over period. Concurrently with this, new screw link couplings were also fitted, and this helped to improve the engines' hauling capabilities. Normally their usual load consisted of eight small coaches, which they managed to handle quite easily. For all this, life on the footplate must have been very arduous, as apart from some meagre 'weatherboards' which were added by the Great Eastern, the driver and fireman were totally exposed to the elements. Fortunately, the Company's colour scheme changed in 1873 when Adams succeeded Johnson as Locomotive Superintendant, and therefore after this, the majority of the class were repainted in black.

In 1866, the nine locomotives were renumbered 91 - 93, and 95 - 100, whilst those that were still in existence twelve years later were altered yet again. This involved the addition of a '0' behind the existing number, but by the time that this was done, there were only six survivors left in service. The first engine to be withdrawn was No. 100, which had ceased working in 1866, and was finally scrapped in the Spring of 1870. After this, the class gradually disappeared, although it wasn't until April 1883 that they actually became extinct. The last one to go was No. 930, which had originally carried the name 'Blackwall', and for a little while after it was taken out of traffic, it was used as a stationary boiler in the wheel shop at Stratford Works. This in fact proved to be the last surviving native London & Blackwall locomotive, as the two goods tanks had both been withdrawn in the early months of 1882. These had been subject to the same renumbering policies as their passenger counterparts, and after being known as 101 and 102 during their middle years, they finally ended up as 1010 and 1020.

Latterly the old passenger locos had shared their duties with some ancient Sharp Stewart express engines, but in the end both types were eventually replaced by a class of 2-4-2 well tank, which had been introduced in 1864, to the design of Robert C. Sinclair. These were strange looking machines with long, low boilers and tall narrow cabs, and because they were built by the firm of Neilson Reid & Co. in Glasgow, they became known colloquially as 'Scotchmen'. All in all, there were twenty of them, and they each weighed 36¼ tons. They measured around 29 ft long and they were fitted with 5' 7" driving wheels. It is believed they were the first tank engines in this country to be equipped with their particular wheel arrangement, and although they were initially painted pea green, they were later turned out in the post 1873 Great Eastern livery of black, lined out with red.

The same year that saw the demise of the indigenous 2-4-0 goods tanks, also witnessed the completion of a Midland Railway freight branch, which led from the eastern end of the Blackwall system, and provided access to Poplar Dock. This started from Poplar Junction which was situated to the east of Prestons Road overbridge, and continued in a south-easterly direction before terminating at a large depot beside the Thames. The branch diverged from the main line a little short of the original Poplar passenger station, which had been abandoned around 1845, and the former 'south' platform was used to accommodate one of the new establishment's buildings. Beyond this, adjacent to the west side of Brunswick Street, the Company built a red brick pump house, which together with the structure erected on the old station site bore a very strong likeness to the Midland's City Goods Depot in Royal Mint Street. Once all the necessary constructional work had been completed, the branch was opened on the 1st of December 1882.

A few years later, the same company opened a coal yard on the north side of the main line at West India Docks. This was provided with sidings at both street and viaduct level, and these were connected to each other by means of a wagon hoist. In 1914, the Midland introduced a tiny four-wheeled battery-electric loco to the depot, and this was used for shunting purposes well into the post-nationalisation period. In more recent times it was known as B. E. L. No. 1, and its great advantage over a steam engine was that it could be transported on a hoist without any difficulty whatsoever. When its days of usefulness were deemed to be over, it was sent to a scrapyard near Brunswick Junction, where it was finally broken up in the April of 1965. B. E. L. No. 1 was an unusual machine and its demise was a great pity, but nevertheless a similar loco, built by the North Stafford Railway in 1917, is now preserved in the National Railway Museum at York.

After the opening of the Midland route to Poplar Dock, the next major development was another goods depot, but this time it was at the opposite end of the main line. It took the shape of a huge complex on the south side of Commercial Road, which was served by a short branch from Christian Street Junction, between Shadwell and Leman Street stations.

It owed its origins to the East & West India Docks Company, who approached the L. T. & S. R. with a view to having a direct link between their new Tilbury Docks and Central London. These docks had been proposed in response to competition from other organisations further upstream, because the Company's existing facilities were becoming unsuitable for modern shipping. When they first applied for a rail connection, the L.T. & S.R. were somewhat unenthusiastic, but after a degree of internal bickering they finally agreed to support the scheme.

Between them, the two organisations drew up the plans for an ambitious London depot to deal solely with the traffic from Tilbury, and the design for this was sanctioned by both A. L. Stride, and the Dock Company's engineer Mr. A. Manning. Once the necessary Parliamentary Authority was granted in 1882, its construction started almost immediately, and soon the great project began to take shape.

From the junction with the main line, the tracks were carried on a curving brick viaduct, and were taken across Backchurch Lane and Hooper Street by means of iron bridges. The depot itself, which was bounded to the west by Lambeth Street, and to the east by Gower's Walk, had facilities at both rail and street level, but of all this, the most dominant feature was a huge four-storeyed warehouse, which had been constructed by the well known firm of J. Mowlem & Co.

The erection of this edifice took rather longer than anticipated, and it was still incomplete when the rest of the depot was opened on the 17th of April 1886. This had been timed to coincide with the ceremonial inauguration of the Tilbury Docks, and the slow progress of the warehouse project engendered a dispute between the parties concerned. Although the Railway claimed that they were not tied to a construction deadline, they nevertheless felt obliged to save face, and for this reason they provided temporary accommodation in an old Hooper Street wool warehouse which they had bought from Messrs. Hyatt Parker & Co.

The initial agreement between its promoters had a clause by which the Dock Company guaranteed that the L. T. & S. R. would convey a minimum annual tonnage of 200,000 tons between Tilbury and Commercial Road, and this they would pay for at a price of 4/6d per ton. They also undertook to finance any deficit at the same rate, on the understanding that this would be minus the cost of carriage, and also the toll paid to the Great Eastern for the use of the approach tracks on the Blackwall viaduct. Over the years that followed, the actual details of this were amended, but the basic contract remained the same, and at various times it became the source of much aggravation between the two organisations.

For their part of the deal, the L. T. & S. R. promised to lease the warehouse to the Dock Company for 99 years, and this agreement became a reality when the building was finally completed in the August of 1887.

Unfortunately the heavy traffic that was expected failed to materialise, and this, together with the massive cost of constructing the facilities at Tilbury, brought the East & West India Docks Company into the hands of the receivers. Help came in 1888 however, when they amalgamated with the owners of St. Katherines further upstream, and thus formed a new partnership known as the London & India Docks Joint Committee.

For most of its life, Commercial Road Depot failed to live up to the aspirations of its creators, and the amount of business that it dealt with in no way justified its lavish proportions. Nevertheless, the L. T. & S. R. were still proud of their achievement, and because of this they named one of their 4-4-2 tank locomotives in its honour. This was originally No. 42, but in 1911 the name was transferred to No. 22, which had previously been known as 'East Horndon'.

Because of the additional traffic anticipated after the opening of Commercial Road Depot, the Great Eastern approached the directors of the Blackwall Company to finance another widening of their viaduct, and this they agreed to do. They duly presented a Bill for this purpose in 1886, but as in the past they had difficulty in finding the required capital. This time it took them nearly four years to raise enough money, and even after their target had been achieved, they still allowed another twelve months to elapse before they appointed a contractor. Eventually the job got under way, but it wasn't until the March of 1896 that an additional down line was opened between Fenchurch Street and Stepney.

Considering the amount of work involved, the men employed on the project did very well, and the lengthy time taken for its completion can only be attributed to inefficiency on behalf of the management. Apart from the prime task of widening the track bed, they also had a lot of station alterations to make, and before the scheme was finished, both Leman Street and Shadwell had been totally rebuilt.

The style of architecture employed for the new structures was typical of the Great Eastern suburban stations of their period, with substantial red-brick buildings and long platform canopies. Shadwell was provided with a new covered way from the 1st of August 1895, which replaced the original one, and thus allowed a better interchange with the East London Line. Five years later, on the 1st of July 1900, the station was renamed 'Shadwell & St. George's East'.

Once all the necessary work had been completed, the trains that were booked to run non-stop between Fenchurch Street and Stepney were routed via the fast lines on the north side of the viaduct, whilst the local services were diagrammed to use those to the south. The stations at Leman Street and Shadwell only had platforms on these tracks, and therefore were only used by the Great Eastern and Blackwall stoppers. The L. T. & S. R. never served either of these, although they'd always called at Stepney since their earliest days, and also began to use Burdett Road after the 1st of November 1891.

Whilst the job of widening the viaduct was in its infancy, a collision occurred at Leman Street which injured about fifty people. This happened on an August Sunday in 1892, when an up Great Eastern passenger train was struck head-on by a light engine, just as it was about to stop at the station. The time was around 11.10 pm, and the driver of a late night working from Forest Gate was in the process of braking, when to his horror he saw an L. T. & S. R. loco approaching him on the same line. Although it was travelling at a fair speed, the crew of this machine also managed to apply their brakes, but not in time to prevent it from ploughing into the oncoming engine. Fortunately nobody was killed, and the majority of victims only suffered from bad cuts and bruises.

Earlier that year, the Great Eastern decided to withdraw its shuttle-service between Fenchurch Street and Bow, which it had inherited from the North London in 1869. Because they wished to retain the connection with the Broad Street line, they resited their own Bow

Road station, and joined it to the existing North London establishment by means of a covered way. This must have been quite a major undertaking, as the new buildings were much more substantial than their predecessors, and the viaduct had to be widened slightly to accommodate them.

The new station was built to the north of the original, and had its entrance directly across the road from the one it replaced. Its most prominent architectural features were the distinctive stairways which stood at either end of the long, curving platforms, and these, in common with the rest of the main structure, were built of red brick. The pair at the City end descended to the booking hall, whilst those nearer to Stratford led through to the North London. All their inside walls were lined with glazed white tiles, and their roofs were made of glass, held in place by a light metal framework. The platforms themselves were covered for their entire length by the type of canopy then most favoured for Great Eastern suburban stations, and although this afforded the maximum protection from the weather, it also had the effect of blocking out a lot of the natural light. The lengthy sections of retaining wall that supported these awnings were of brick construction, although the attendant waiting rooms and suchlike had fronts that were made of wood. The building at street level stood on the north side of Bow Road, east of the viaduct, and typified the urban station of its period. It had two double doorways and a large window, and each of these was complemented by an ornamental keystone set within a segmental arch. There was also a triangular pediment above each entrance, but apart from these, there was little superficial embellishment. Nevertheless, its design was far from being unattractive, and indeed the new frontage was pleasing to the eye.

The Fenchurch Street to Bow shuttle ran for the last time on the 3rd of April 1892, and the new Bow Road station opened the following day. After this, the 1 in 99 spur which joined the North London with the Blackwall Extension Railway was closed to regular passenger traffic.

This was the second physical connection between these two companies to be lost within two years, as the Broad Street to Blackwall service had been cut back to Poplar from the 1st of July 1890. By this time, the number of excursionists using Brunswick Wharf had dropped drastically, and the whitebait suppers which had been so popular fifty years earlier had become but a memory. Railway developments south of the Thames had eroded much of the river traffic, and the Blackwall terminus itself had settled down to a much quieter existence than before. The Great Eastern had noted this decline in fortunes some years earlier, when they reduced the Sunday service on the line to half-hourly from October 1883, and the through trains from Broad Street were withdrawn simply because they had ceased to be economically viable. A month or so after they stopped operating, the Great Eastern removed the points, and the North London erected buffer stops on their side of the former junction, and therefore a link which had been in existence since 1852 had become permanently severed.

Another blow to the Railway's river interest came with the passing of the Thames Tunnel Act in 1897. This authorised the construction of a pedestrian subway between Cubitt Town and Greenwich, which would replace the ferries, and establish a better link for the estimated 1,300,000 people who travelled each year between the two districts. For some time there had been public complaints about the bad lighting conditions on the stairs leading to the North Greenwich landing stage, and the crossings were inclined to be unreliable and even dangerous, particularly when they were affected by bad weather. The Great Eastern naturally disapproved of the scheme, but finally agreed to withdraw their objection when they were offered a sum of £8,000 in compensation. The new Greenwich Foot Tunnel opened on the 4th of August 1902, and the ferries were withdrawn two months later on the 31st of October.

Back in 1889, a new class of engines was introduced that were destined to have a long association with the Blackwall services. These were the 'E22' type 0-6-0 tanks which were designed for the Great Eastern by James Holden. They were fitted with 4' coupled wheels and two 14" x 20" inside cylinders, and their weight in full working order was 36 tons 11 cwt. Their length from end to end was 27' 2" and they were painted in the splendid Great Eastern livery of royal blue. Initially there were only ten of them, and these were numbered 150 - 159, but four years later, Stratford Works turned out another batch which they designated 245 - 254. Once these had been completed, the class finally comprised of twenty engines, and because the running number of the first one was 150, they were sometimes referred to as the '150 Type'.

They were the smallest of the 0-6-0Ts to be designed by Holden, and some of them that operated to Blackwall had the leading sections of their coupling rods removed, which technically converted them to 2-4-0Ts. They continued in service for many years, and the last one was not scrapped until 1956.

By 1902, the patronage of the Blackwall services had tailed off to such an extent that the trains were reduced to three every hour. This was the beginning of a steady decline which accelerated with the introduction of electric trams along Commercial Road in 1906. After this, the line began to lose its popularity, and the installation of shipping office telephones meant that it was no longer necessary for messengers to use it when communicating between the City and the Docks. Around this time the decrepit overall roof at Blackwall station was beginning to look dangerous, and it was therefore dismantled and replaced by conventional umbrella type awnings. Stepney's own little railway, which had once been regarded as a main line, had now become downgraded to a branch, whilst the L.T.& S.R. presence at Fenchurch Street continued to grow in its importance.

It was always a cause of concern to this Company that they were reliant upon someone else's City terminus for the success of their operations, and at various times in their existence, proposals had been made to build one of their own. By the later 'Nineties, the congestion at Fenchurch Street had again become so acute that the L. T. & S. R. approached the Metropolitan District Railway, with a view to co-sponsoring a line which would connect the two systems together. After an agreement had been reached, the companies applied for the necessary Parliamentary Authority, and an Act was passed on the 6th of August 1897 which sanctioned its construction. The line was known as The Whitechapel & Bow Joint Railway, and it cost £1,200,000 to complete. It left the L. T. & S. R. at Campbell Road, which was a quarter of a mile east of Gas Factory Junction, and then descended on a short, sharp gradient of 1 in 45 to reach its first intermediate station. From this initial section, the line continued in a shallow tunnel beneath the main road until it reached Whitechapel, where it made an end-on connection with the existing tracks. It was built by using the 'cut-and-cover' method, and whilst construction was still in its early stages, a section of the Blackwall Extension viaduct south of Bow Road had to be demolished in order for the men to tunnel underneath it. To enable this to be done with the minimum disruption to the Great Eastern services, a temporary bridge of wood and iron was erected, and after this the old one was blown up by engineers. Anything that might have been left at track level of the original 1876 Bow Road station probably disappeared at this time, although the former booking office, albeit much disfigured still survives to the present day. Once the job had been completed, the viaduct was rebuilt and its temporary replacement was dismantled.

Although the Whitechapel & Bow Joint Railway never provided the L. T. & S. R. with its own City terminus, it did at least cater for the needs of many passengers from their inner-suburban stations, and therefore helped to take some of the pressure away from Fenchurch Street.

Despite its continuing success, it was always assumed that one day the L. T. & S. R. would be absorbed by the Great Eastern, but in the February of 1911, the Company's Chairman, Arthur Lewis Stride, announced that following his forthcoming retirement, the line was to be taken over by the Midland Railway. This came as quite a surprise at the time, as the Midland seemed one of the most unlikely organisations to achieve a substantial foothold in the East End, but the circumstances were in their favour, and following a tempting financial bid, the aging chief of the L. T. & S. R., who was in failing health anyway, agreed that his line should be sold.

The Midland had gained direct access to the Tilbury system in July 1894, when the Tottenham & Forest Gate Joint Railway was opened between South Tottenham and Woodgrange Park. Although the Great Eastern was strongly opposed to the sale, they agreed to drop their objections after they received various offers of appeasement, and the Midland's Bill of acquisition received the Royal Assent on the 7th of August 1912. Nevertheless, despite this apparent settlement, the Great Eastern no doubt obtained a great deal of pleasure by informing the Midland that a class of eight large 4-6-4 tank locomotives, which had just been delivered for the Southend services, were too heavy for the Blackwall viaduct, and therefore had to be banned from using Fenchurch Street.

To the casual observer, the most noticeable change that was brought about by the takeover was the colour scheme of the ex-L.T.& S.R. locomotives. Whereas in the past they had been painted green, or latterly in a shade of lavender known as 'french grey', the Midland began to outshop them in their standard livery of crimson lake. As the engines were repainted they also lost their names, which was a great pity, as this little feature had given them a lot of charm and character.

On the 28th of December 1913, a few months before the outbreak of The Great War, the Millwall Extension Railway finally lost its Sunday passenger service, which rather surprisingly had operated in comparative isolation for over four years. The Sunday trains on the Blackwall line itself had actually been withdrawn from the 4th of October 1908, and on the following 26th of January, the East End News contained this paragraph which announced that the Company were about to cut some of their fares by between fifteen and twenty per cent:-

"The Great Eastern Railway have suffered severely through the coming of the motor 'bus and electric car. The reduction on March 1 will affect the Blackwall to Fenchurch Street line, which has been very hardly hit during the past two or three years when the City first became within speedy access by motor and electric car. Now that the road has so outdone the rail, I doubt very much, even with

reduced fares, if the old Blackwall line will every regain its pristine popularity."

With the onset of the War, and the guns of the Western Front demanding their evil quota of human sacrifice, the Great Eastern decided to close some of their stations to release more men for the trenches, and two of these were on the former Blackwall system. These were Leman Street and Shadwell & St. Georges East, which together with a number of similar establishments on the approaches to Liverpool Street, were closed from the 22nd of May 1916. Around the same time, the train services to Blackwall and North Greenwich were reduced to half-hourly, although by this period a very few people were using them anyway. An article in the East London Advertiser of the 8th of April, bemoaned many of the imminent closures, but also made the following scathing comments:-

"The closing of Leman Street, in Whitechapel, and Shadwell Stations should have been done a long time ago, the traffic at these stations being trifling compared with the cost of their maintenance. Besides, both districts are better served by 'buses and tramcars."

Apart from these apparently unloved stations, another wartime casualty was the interchange facility at Bow Road, where the covered way was closed and sealed off at the beginning of 1917.

As it turned out, this was the only significant piece of rationalisation which remained permanent, as both Shadwell and Leman Street stations were re-opened from the 5th of May and 1st of July 1919 respectively, and the Blackwall trains were restored to their old frequency of one every fifteen minutes. Perhaps this decision on behalf of the Great Eastern to restore such an intensive service on a line whose fortunes were then so sadly in decline, remains somewhat of a mystery, particularly as the trains had previously been reduced to three an hour, as long ago as 1902. In his book 'First and Last Loves', the late Sir John Betjeman gave this short account of what it was like to travel on the line during its twilight days:-

"...Those frequent and quite empty trains of the Blackwall Railway ran from a special platform at Fenchurch Street. I remember them well. Like stage coaches they rumbled slowly past East-End chimney pots, wharves and shipping, stopping at black and empty stations, till they came to a final halt at Blackwall. When one emerged there was nothing to see but a cobbled quay and a vast stretch of windswept water."

In another of his works, 'London's Historic Railway Stations', Sir

John also recalled this:-

"...I remember the delightful old fashioned rolling stock and once travelled on it First Class, where the seats were cushions of black leather with buttons, and the carriage door had so rarely been opened that the compartment smelt and felt like the interior of a family brougham left forgotten in the stables."

A similar state of affairs existed on the branch to North Greenwich, where the tired little engines still puffed their weary way to and from the empty riverside terminus. On their journey they paused at the two desolate intermediate stations, where only a handful of dockers continued to notice their presence, and hardly anyone bothered to get on or off. Here the demand was so low that the trains retained their half-hourly wartime schedule, and unlike their neighbours on the route to Blackwall, they were never restored to their former frequency.

Throughout its entire existence, the Millwall Extension Line had always been managed by both the Railway and the dock organisations, although over the years the latter had been affected by a number of changes. Firstly the old E.& W. India Docks Company became incorporated into the London & India Docks Joint Committee in 1888, and then in 1901, the name was again altered by having the words 'Joint Committee' replaced by the more succinct 'Company'. This is how it remained until 1909, when together with the nearby Millwall Dock it was swallowed up by the newly formed Port of London Authority.

It was after the P. L. A. took control that the decision was made to scrap the old engines and replace them with three highly unsuitable steam railmotors which they purchased secondhand from the Great Western Railway. By this time the little Manning Wardles were over forty years old, and were virtually worn out. In their day they were claimed to be the smallest standard gauge passenger locomotives in the country, and the branch lost much of its character when they were all withdrawn in 1922. Two of the railmotors were built in 1904 at Swindon Works and were fitted with 0-4-0 driving bogies, whilst the other was an unwanted cast-off from the Welsh Valleys. This vehicle had been built for the Port Talbot Railway by Beyer Peacock & Co. Ltd. in 1906, and although it originally had an engine section with an 0-6-0 wheel base, it was later converted to a 2-4-0. All of the units concerned were specially reduced in weight, but nevertheless many of the line's bridges had to be strengthened before any of them were allowed to enter service. The overall length of these railmotors also made them tight on curves, and because of this, the facing points had to be fitted with 45 ft locking bars. The work necessary to bring the branch up to this shabby new standard took around two years to complete, and during this period the services were maintained by some small Great Eastern 0-4-0 saddle tanks.

By the time the railmotors finally began to work the line, the London & Blackwall Company had at long last officially ceased to exist. This was after the 1st of January 1923, when as a result of a Parliamentary Act two years earlier, it became part of the huge network that was owned by the London & North Eastern Railway. For well over eighty years the Blackwall organisation had remained nominally independent, despite being the subject of a lease agreement since 1866, and an unsuccessful bid by the Great Eastern to buy it outright in 1898. The Railway Act of 1921 not only prompted the takeover of the entire Great Eastern system by the L. N. E. R., it also created the London Midland & Scottish Railway, who absorbed the old L. T. & S. R. route amongst many others.

During the years that followed, the importance of the services to Tilbury and Southend grew out of all proportion to those of the former Great Eastern, and in time, just like a baby cuckoo in a nest, they finally inherited the entire terminus.

	eve.	eve.	eve.	eve.	eve.	eve.	eve.	eve.	eve	eve.	eve.	eve.	eve.	eve.	eve.	eve.	eve.	eve.	eve.
Blackwall ... ...dep.	2 5	2 20	2 35	2 50	3 5	3 20	3 35	3 49	4 5	4 20	4 35	4 50	5 5	5 18	5 35	5 50	6 5	6 20	6 35
Poplar	2 6	2 21	2 36	2 51	3 6	3 21	3 36	3 50	4 6	4 21	4 36	4 51	5 6	5 19	5 36	5 51	6 6	6 21	6 36
North Greenwich ... (Cubitt Town)	1 51	2 6	2 23	2 37	2 51	3 6	3 23	3 37	3 51	4 6	4 23	4 37	4 51	5 6	5 23	5 37	5 51	6 6	6 23
Millwall Docks	1 54	2 9	2 26	2 40	2 54	3 9	3 26	3 40	3 54	4 9	4 26	4 40	4 54	5 9	5 26	5 40	5 54	6 9	6 26
South Dock...	1 57	2 12	2 29	2 43	2 57	3 12	3 29	3 43	3 57	4 12	4 29	4 43	4 57	5 12	5 29	5 43	5 57	6 12	6 29
Millwall Junc.... arr.	2 0	2 16	2 33	2 46	3 0	3 16	3 33	3 46	4 0	4 16	4 33	4 46	5 0	5 16	5 33	5 46	6 0	6 16	6 33
Millwall Junction ...dep.	2 8	2 23	2 38	2 53	3 8	3 23	3 38	3 52	4 8	4 23	4 38	4 53	5 8	5 21	5 38	5 53	6 8	6 23	6 38
West India Docks	2 10	2 25	2 40	2 55	3 10	3 25	3 40	3 54	4 10	4 25	4 40	4 55	5 10	5 23	5 40	5 55	6 10	6 25	6 40
Limehouse	2 12	2 27	2 42	2 57	3 12	3 27	3 42	3 56	4 12	4 27	4 42	4 57	5 12	5 25	5 42	5 57	6 12	6 27	6 42
Stepney	2 14	2 29	2 44	2 59	3 14	3 29	3 44	3 58	4 14	4 29	4 44	4 59	5 14	5 27	5 44	5 59	6 14	6 29	6 44
Shadwell&St.George's,E	2 17	2 32	2 47	3 2	3 17	3 32	3 47	4 1	4 17	4 32	4 47	5 2	5 17	5 30	5 47	6 2	6 17	6 32	6 47
Leman Street	2 19	2 34	2 49	3 4	3 19	3 34	3 49	4 3	4 19	4 34	4 49	5 4	5 19	5 32	5 49	6 4	6 19	6 34	6 49
Fenchurch Street arr.	2 21	2 36	2 51	3 6	3 21	3 36	3 51	4 5	4 21	4 36	4 51	5 6	5 21	5 34	5 51	6 6	6 21	6 36	6 51

	eve.	eve.	eve.	eve.		eve.		eve.		eve.		eve.		eve.		eve.		eve.	eve.
Blackwall ... ...dep.	6 50	7 4	7 20	7 48	...	8 20	...	8 50	...	9 20	...	9 50	...	1018	...	1050	...	1120	1148
Poplar	6 51	7 5	7 21	7 49	...	8 21	...	8 51	...	9 21	...	9 51	...	1019	...	1051	...	1121	1149
North Greenwich ... (Cubitt Town)	6 45	...	7 7	7 37	...	8 7	...	8 37	...	9 7	...	9 37	...	10 7	...	1037	...	11 7	1137
Millwall Docks	6 48	...	7 10	7 40	...	8 10	...	8 40	...	9 10	...	9 40	...	1010	...	1040	...	1110	1140
South Dock	...	...	...	...	...	...	...	...	...	...	...	...	...	...	...	...	...	...	...
Millwall Junc.... arr.	6 52	...	7 15	7 45	...	8 15	.	8 45	...	9 15	...	9 45	...	1015	...	1045	...	1115	1145
Millwall Junction ...dep.	6 53	7 7	7 23	7 51	...	8 23	...	8 53	...	9 23	...	9 53	...	1021	...	1053	...	1123	1151
West India Docks	6 55	7 9	7 25	7 53	...	8 25	...	8 55	...	9 25	...	9 55	...	1023	...	1055	...	1125	1153
Limehouse	6 57	7 11	7 27	7 55	...	8 27	...	8 57	...	9 27	...	9 57	...	1025	...	1057	...	1127	1155
Stepney	6 59	7 13	7 29	7 57	...	8 29	...	8 59	...	9 29	...	9 59	...	1027	..	1059	.:	1129	1157
Shadwell&St.George's,E.	7 2	7 16	7 32	8 0	...	8 32	...	9 2	..	9 32	...	10 2	...	1030	..	11 2	...	1132	12 0
Leman Street	7 4	7 18	7 34	8 2	...	8 34	...	9 4	...	9 34	...	10 4	..	1032	...	11 4	...	1134	12 2
Fenchurch Street arr.	7 6	7 20	7 36	8 4	...	8 36	...	9 6	...	9 36	...	10 6	..	1034	...	11 6	...	1136	12 4

On Week Days, South Dock Station is closed at 6.29 p.m. and entirely on Sundays.

The Free Tunnel for Foot Passengers between North Greenwich (Cubitt Town) and Greenwich is open day and night. The northern entrance to the Tunnel is near to North Greenwich Station.

THROUGH TICKETS are issued between South Dock, Millwall Docks, and North Greenwich on the one hand, and on the other **hand, all Stations on the Blackwall** Line, Fenchurch Street to Blackwall and Bow Road inclusive; Stratford **and all Stations to Palace** Gates, Southend-on-Sea, Burnham-on-Crouch, and Southminster. Stations on the East **London Line via Shadwell,** Stations on the **Midland Railway** (London Tilbury **and** Southend Section), including Gravesend, via Stepney. * Saturdays only. b Not on Saturdays.

EXTRACT FROM G.E.R. TIMETABLE: AUGUST 1914

A CHRONICLE OF CLOSURES

The first noticeable change after the L. N. E. R. took control of the former Blackwall system was purely a superficial one. It concerned the station at Stepney, which for some reason best known to themselves, they decided to rename 'Stepney East' on the 1st of July, 1923. Presumably the idea behind this was to avoid confusion with Stepney Green on the Whitechapel & Bow Line, but as they both had different names in the first place, the exercise seems a little pointless.

Other than this however, everything carried on much as it had since before the War, with passenger services to Blackwall and North Greenwich still poorly patronised and running almost empty. On the erstwhile main line the old 'E22' tank engines, which had been re-classified as 'J65s' by the L. N. E. R. were occasionally joined by members of the 'F7' class, which were lightweight 2-4-2 tanks introduced in 1909 to the design of James Holden. In fact, these were the smallest of the many 2-4-2T classes that the Great Eastern had built, and their total weight in full working order was a mere 45 tons, 14 cwt. Because they had large cabs with an abundance of glazing at the front and rear, they were known to their drivers as 'Crystal Palaces', although in more rural areas they were also nick-named 'Glasshouses'. Their appearance on Blackwall duties was reasonably uncommon, although their heavier sisters of the 'F4' class could often be seen heading the services from Fenchurch Street to Stratford and beyond. Another type of loco that was used on these trains was the 'N7' class 0-6-2 tanks, which were designed by A. J. Hill, and built by the Great Eastern from 1914 onwards. These were the engines that were much associated with the so-called 'Jazz Services' which operated from the west side of Liverpool Street station in the early 1920s, but they were also fairly widespread throughout the rest of the suburban system. They became a familiar sight, working the line through to Bow Road, although at 64 tons, 17 cwt, they were far too heavy to be allowed on the Blackwall branch itself. The 'N7s' were truly fine machines, and they gave sterling service to the people of East London until the last one was withdrawn in 1962. Fortunately No.999E, one of a later batch which was built by the L. N. E. R., has been preserved and can be seen at the East Anglian Railway Museum, Chappel & Wakes Colne, near

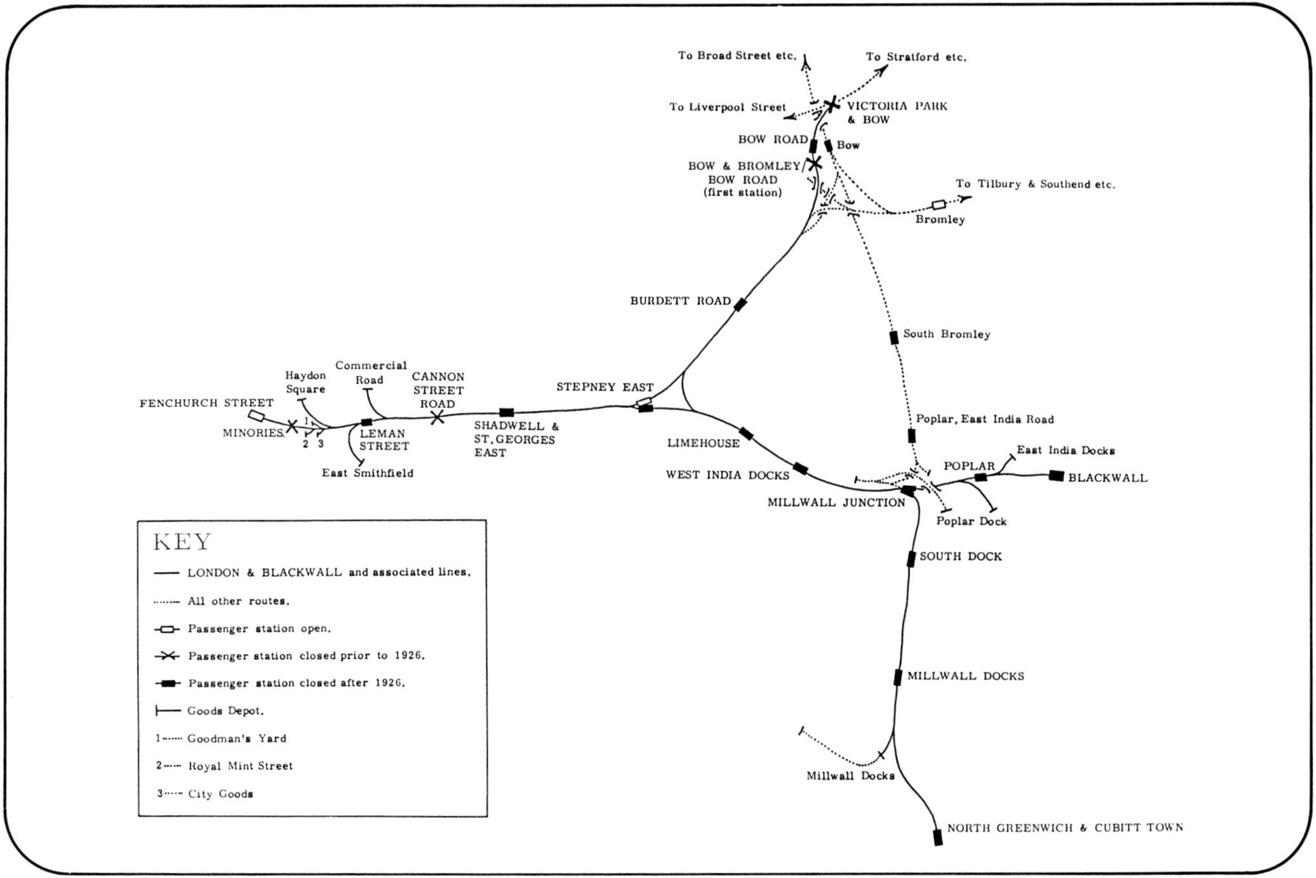

THE LONDON & BLACKWALL SYSTEM 1923 - 1950.

Colchester Essex.

By now the ex-Great Western railmotors were finally working on the North Greenwich branch, but their performance was far from perfect, and they did nothing to save the line from impending extinction. Apart from anything else, their unwieldy bulk caused them to foul objects by the trackside, and all-in-all, the vehicles proved to be a lot more trouble than they were worth.

It must have come as no surprise on the 23rd of March 1926, when closure notices were pasted up at all the relevant stations, stating that the two branches only had three more months to live. The date that was planned for their withdrawal was the 30th of June, but fate stepped in, and the end came quicker than anyone expected.

1926 was of course the year of the General Strike, and because of this, the last trains actually operated on the 3rd of May. The following day however, the driver and fireman rostered to work the early North Greenwich shift reported for duty as normal, but after they were met at the dock gates by a group of pickets, they decided to change their minds and go home.

Unlike more recent closures, there were no railway enthusiasts wallowing in the last rites, nor were there any engines sporting wreaths on their smokebox doors. Even the comparative few who then made a hobby out of collecting tickets were robbed of the opportunity of purchasing a few last issues, and the final trains departed with no cheering crowds or exploding detonators to mark their passing. In fact, with Churchill's armoured cars trundling menacingly along Commercial Road, the people of the East End must have had other things on their minds at the time, and most of them probably never even noticed the line had closed.

Once the strike was over, things got back to normal, but of course the Blackwall and North Greenwich passenger trains had ceased to run for ever. Admittedly, the tracks were still used for freight traffic, but it didn't take long for a general air of neglect to set in, and soon the old structures began to look rather dowdy. The majority of goods workings approached the route from the Salmon's Lane direction, and after passing under the gantry signal box at Limehouse Junction, they continued on their journey eastward. On their way they rattled through the dark and deserted little stations at Limehouse and West India Docks, where the sagging wooden platforms and broken windows created an atmosphere of creeping dereliction. After these were closed, all their nameboards and signs were removed, and the places where they were once fixed glared out as vaguely cleaner patches against the rest of the blackened, peeling paintwork.

Just beyond West India Docks, the goods trains passed the Midland coal depot on the down side, and then began to descend into the cutting which took them through to Millwall Junction. On their way, they probably whistled for West India Dock Bank Signal Box, where heavily laden westbound freights would sometimes have to wait for a banking engine to help them with the climb up to the viaduct. Many of these would be carrying the Elder & Fyffe banana traffic, which originated from the south side of the East India Docks, and was destined for various places throughout the country. These trains were normally operated as required, and generally consisted of around 35 to 45 loaded box-vans.

Shortly before reaching Millwall Junction, eastbound workings would pass a large seventeen-road marshalling yard on their down side, which belonged to the former North London system, and was known as Harrow Lane Sidings. This great complex of tracks was entered from the Broad Street line, although a connecting spur to the Blackwall system had existed since 1873.

At Millwall Junction itself, the tall signal box stood within an impressive array of pointwork, with the lines from the North London to the left, and a combined engine and carriage shed to the right. The old station remained open for freight traffic for a little while after the passenger services were withdrawn, but it finally closed completely from the 14th of November 1927. Despite this, its appearance remained little changed, and as late as 1936 the place was still virtually intact, with all its awnings, lamps and general fittings. Behind its down platform was positioned a small loco yard which was owned by the L. M. S., and once provided a home for their 0-6-0 tank engine No. 11271. This machine was the second of a series of ten light dock shunters which were built at Derby Works between 1928 and 1929 to the design of Sir Henry Fowler. She was destined to have a long career, and wasn't actually withdrawn until the early 1960s. However, it's only fair to say that by this time, she had long since vacated her former stamping ground, and was in fact shedded at Fleetwood in Lancashire.

Just inside the P. L. A.'s boundary fence at Millwall Junction could be seen the Saxby & Farmer signal cabin which was known, rather confusingly, as West India Docks. This was the first box on the North Greenwich branch, although its function had always been in connection with freight traffic rather than passenger. Beyond this, the line curved sharply to the south, and finally disappeared behind a succession of tall warehouses.

After passing Millwall, the trains rumbled under the Prestons Road overbridge and then reached Poplar Junction. Here the signal box was a fairly standard Great Eastern design, and had wooden upper parts supported by a brick base. It stood on the up side of the former main line, and overlooked the spot where the old Midland Railway's dock branch diverged to the right. Here could be seen the long abandoned platforms of the original Poplar station, which despite their many years of disuse, were still in a reasonable state of preservation. The one on the down side was admittedly very overgrown by this time, but its opposite number was kept in better condition, as it accommodated one of the buildings associated with the goods depot. Whatever the precise use of this structure was remains somewhat of a mystery, but its general shape and styling suggests that it was in some way connected with the nearby pump-house, which stood on the up side of the branch itself, immediately before the Brunswick Street overbridge. Both buildings were constructed of red and blue bricks, and were typical examples of Midland Railway architecture. With their characteristic windows and other features, they were very similar to the City Goods Station in Royal Mint Street, and they also resembled the majority of other depot structures which existed throughout the system of their former owner. Beyond the overbridge was positioned the Poplar Dock signal box, which again was purely 'Midland' with wooden slatted sides and decorative finials at either end of its roof.

Back on the erstwhile main line however, the trains passed beneath Brunswick Street, and then came to the later Poplar station. This was situated in a brick-lined cutting, and was served by an entrance on the east side of the road. The wooden street-level building stretched the entire width of the bridge, and led on to the two glazed and covered stairways which descended to the platforms. Beneath the stairs on the down side was a door belonging to a coal store, whilst opposite this, on the other platform was a similar entrance which provided access to a lamp room. Both platforms were covered for about half their length by valanced awnings, although these were of two different styles. the one on the westbound side was of a typically Great Eastern 'zig-zag' type, and was very similar to those employed on many of the suburban stations out of Liverpool Street, such as Bishopsgate, Bethnal Green and Globe Road. A canopy of this design was also used above the entrance to Fenchurch Street after the original had been taken down in the 1860's, and indeed at one time it was one of the most common types to be found in the East End. By way of contrast however, the one on the down side at Poplar was rather less elaborate, and it was fitted with a very ordinary, undistinguished form of valancing. Just clear of this stood a small wooden building, which was reputedly used as a station master's office. This little hut, together with the majority of other station fittings was demolished around 1936, although it is believed that some of the awnings disappeared shortly after closure.

East of Poplar could be found the wooden Great Eastern signal box of Brunswick Junction, where the East India Dock branch diverged towards the left. Opposite this, on the south side of the old main line, ran an 8' gauge steam crane which served the dry dock owned by the ship building firm of Green & Silley Weir. The Great Northern depot comprised of eight individual sidings, of which two were fed by means of a headshunt, into a goods shed on the east side of Quixley Street. The yard, which was also connected to the P.L.A. system, was shunted by horses, and because of this a stable existed near its north western boundary.

Once beyond Brunswick Junction, the line continued into Blackwall, although after closure to passengers, this section was generally only used for temporary wagon storage. There was a siding on the up side which terminated in a blank arch beneath East India Dock Wall Road, and above this there were marks on the brickwork which suggested that it could have been the site of the old Blackwall engine shed. This theory was further substantiated by the presence of a brick-based water tower which stood to the north of the line, although at the time some people believed that this structure had North London origins.

After this bridge, the tracks veered vaguely northwards past a small hut which contained a six-lever ground frame, and then continued for a few more yards into Blackwall itself. After it was no longer required for its intended purpose, part of the palatial main building was used to house two railway families, and one of these belonged to the old station foreman. Between them they must have had the most sumptuous railway accommodation in the East End and today such a property, with almost unequalled views over the Thames, would be worth a small fortune. On a wall adjoining the station entrance was positioned a plaque which commemorated Captain John Smith's epic voyage from Blackwall to America in 1607, which resulted in him founding the colony of Virginia.

Because of the cramped facilities at the terminus, the down track from Brunswick Junction was sometimes used for two-way running, although this was generally only necessary during shunting operations. The station itself remained little altered after closure, except that the nameboards and platform lamps were removed. However, it didn't take long for the demolition men to start on some of the line's other buildings, presumably because they were in a fairly dangerous condition by this time. The platforms and buildings at Limehouse were the first to disappear completely around 1929. About the same time the signal box at the east end of West India Docks up platform was also taken down although the station itself survived for another two or three years.

Despite the existence of virtually parallel bus and tram services, the L. N. E. R. considered re-opening the route to passengers during the early 1930's, and for this purpose two five-coach articulated sets were tested on the branch. Unfortunately it was found that these vehicles, which were known as 'Quint Arts', were too wide for the clearance between the tracks, and at certain places they were actually found to be unsafe when they passed each other. Therefore after a few trial runs, the coaches were returned to their sidings, and the idea was abandoned.

Some of the old coaching stock which had formerly operated on the Blackwall services was probably used, prior to scrapping, on the East End school excursions which ran during the summer holidays and gave local boys and girls the opportunity of a few days in the country. To travel on these, the children paid a weekly penny or so to their teacher, until they reached a target of 1/6d, and when the time came, they were taken in special trains to either Loughton or Chingford. They received quite a good deal for their savings as well, because once the money had been paid, it entitled them to make a return journey every alternate weekday for a total of three weeks. The trains themselves operated from Fenchurch Street, and called at most of the inner suburban stations, before proceeding non-stop to Loughton. Having arrived, some of the children got out, whilst others stayed on and made the trip back to Stratford, and thence round to Chingford via Lea Bridge and Hall Farm Junction. After reaching this final destination, the excited youngsters would be escorted to the outskirts of Epping Forest, where they could sample the delights of Connaught Waters and a refreshing bottle of lemonade at Butler's Retreat.

Apart from these comparatively local runs, some schools arranged more ambitious trips to Southend, although these of course were inclined to be somewhat more expensive, and also less plentiful. This time however, the normal public services were utilised, and reserved compartments were set aside for the children before the trains left the City.

In addition to this schools traffic however, there were of course other excursion trains from Fenchurch Street, although the majority of these operated to destinations on the former L. T. & S. R. system. Probably the best of these from a value point of view was the 6/- inclusive return ticket that could be bought to Ramsgate from either Fenchurch Street, Stepney or Burdett Road. This bargain fare enabled passengers to travel through to Tilbury, and then join the paddle steamer 'Royal Eagle' for a leisurely cruise to the Isle of Thanet. Apart from this, there was also a 2/- evening excursion ticket to Southend, which entitled the passengers to gain free admission to the Kursaal Amusement Park, once they had arrived.

In fact, the 1930's saw the popularity of the former L.T.& S.R. services growing from strength to strength, and a stranger visiting Fenchurch Street during this period could well imagine that he was standing on an L. M. S. station. Of course, there were still the trains out to places such as Ilford, Loughton and North Woolwich, but these were fast becoming insignificant when compared with those which operated to Southend.

To cope with this heavy passenger traffic, the L. M. S. Chief Mechanical Engineer, Mr. W. A. Stanier, introduced a powerful class of thirty-seven 2-6-4 tank locomotives to the line in 1934, which completely dwarfed the engines which worked the local L.N.E.R. services. From end to end they measured 47' 2¾", and their driving wheels had a diameter of 5' 9". They had 3' 3½" carrying wheels front and back, and they were fitted with three 16" x 26" cylinders. Their total weight in working order came to 92 tons 5 cwt, and their large bunkers could carry over three tons of coal. The engines numbered from 2500 to 2536, and their outward appearance was very attractive indeed. In common with all of Stanier's designs, they had gracefully tapered boilers, and the L. M. S. secondary passenger livery of black lined out with red, suited them perfectly. Most of the class remained in service on the line until being ousted by electrification in 1962, and after this they were withdrawn for scrapping. The first one however, was not broken up, and after being stored at various places including Stratford Works, it was finally restored to its original condition and can now be seen alongside 'Thundersley' at the Bressingham Steam Museum in Norfolk.

A couple of years before these machines made their debut, work was started on yet another modernisation scheme for Fenchurch Street. This entailed the replacement of the existing platforms with two new islands, because all of the old ones, with the exception of Number 4, were too short to accommodate modern length trains. Ideally, it would have been better to expand the actual station site itself, but the value of the adjoining properties unfortunately ruled this out. The complete plan was estimated to cost around £250,000, and also included the installation of colour-light signalling all the way through to Bow Junction. The improvements commenced in 1932, and one of the first jobs to be completed was the reorganisation of the booking hall. Here the L. N. E. R. and L. M. S. facilities were combined, and a new parcels office was opened to replace the one on the concourse. Up at track level, the old bookstall which stood beside the entrances to Platforms 1 and 2, was removed to create more space within the circulating area, and the old tea rooms and telegraph office which were adjacent to the north wall were also closed. The other refreshment room which backed onto the main station frontage was rebuilt in the 'Art-Deco' style, and the nearby waiting rooms and toilets also received a similar treatment. The platforms themselves were of course much longer than the majority of their predecessors, and the approach tracks which served them were also simplified. The shortest of the islands measured 550 ft, and this was positioned between the two slow lines on the south side of the viaduct. This became known as platforms 1 and 2, and was intended for the use of the L. N. E. R. services. The other one, which had a total length of 750 ft was reserved for the L. M. S., and its two faces received the numbers of 3 and 4. The old barriers were replaced by wrought-iron ones which were arranged in a similar fashion to some already in use at Liverpool Street, and these provided alternative exits from all platforms. New train indicators were also installed, and these again resembled their counterparts at Liverpool Street. They were all fitted with dummy clocks which displayed the departure times, and each one had a list of stations which could be set as required by the ticket collector.

Umbrella type awnings were fitted above the two sections of platform which protruded beyond the length of the overall roof, and a new subway was constructed which provided access from both of these islands to the old John Street building. Despite the fact that this entrance was officially renamed 'Crosswall' from the 1st of July 1939, tickets issued there today still bear the suffix 'John Street', although why this should be remains something of a mystery.

The actual work of rebuilding the station was completed by the 29th of April 1935, and this included the installation of the up-to-date signalling equipment. The 140 lever box at Fenchurch Street was in fact brought into use fifteen days earlier, and this, together with modernised panels inside the old cabins at Stepney East and Gas Factory Junction, replaced a total of nine earlier installations. Its predecessor at the City terminus used to stand on a gantry over the up slow line, and this had been fitted with 115 manual levers within a Saxby & Farmer type frame. The new box also straddled above the approach tracks, but instead of semaphores it controlled a succession of four-aspect colour lights, and also a large number of electric point motors.

Unfortunately from this time onwards, the success story of Fenchurch Street was restricted to the services of the L. M. S., and the importance of the L. N. E. R. presence began to fade, as tram and bus competition was proving too much for them, and eventually the decline in patronage started to set in. As an indication of things to come, the L. N. E. R. announced that from the 5th of May 1935, Bow Road station would be closed on Sundays, although at least there would be no other reduction in the services provided.

On the sad little Millwall Extension Railway, it had become virtually impossible to restore the passenger trains even if anybody actually wanted to. In 1929 a section of the formation near South Dock was blown-up to allow dock improvements, and although a new loop was constructed to by-pass this, the tracks were only suitable for freight traffic. At the opposite end of the branch, a section of viaduct south of Glengall Road was demolished in 1937, and a person was killed when one of the arches collapsed. This caused a bit of public interest at the time and questions were asked about it in Parliament, but after the fuss had subsided the line faded into almost total obscurity. The vast proportion of the viaduct survived however, and it can still be seen dissecting the fields of Millwall Park. The little terminus also remained standing, although the site was later redeveloped in 1969. For many years it stayed virtually intact, even down to the canopy, but eventually the whole thing fell into disrepair and had to be demolished. For the majority of its twilight period the building was used for storage, but during its later years it was leased to a boating club. This was the last station to survive on the line, and its loss was a sad one, even if inevitable.

About the same time as the fatal accident at Millwall, the engineers finally removed the redundant branch platforms at Stepney East, whilst further down the line, the station buildings at Poplar received a similar treatment. The awnings and other superfluous trappings at Millwall Junction also probably went at this time, although the main building itself remained until 1965.

With the onset of another world war in 1939, the East Enders rightly began to fear the worst, and the area entered into a period of nightmare bombing raids and tragic loss of life. Whole streets disappeared beneath dusty heaps of rubble, and naturally many railway installations suffered from similar fates. Unfortunately the old Blackwall system, being so close to the docks, was regarded by the Luftwaffe as a prime target, and therefore much of it became the subject of their destructive attentions.

The incidents themselves were numerous, and sometimes resulted in many deaths, but it's only possible to record those which had the most serious effects.

The first station on the line to suffer any significant damage was Burdett Road, which was hit during an air-raid on the 29th of December 1940. Surprisingly it was patched up about a week later, although by this time it was comparatively lightly used, and there was no longer any need for its existence. Its death blow finally came on the 10th of April 1941, when a bomb fell to the east of the viaduct, and destroyed virtually all of the up-side platform buildings. This rendered the entire structure unsafe, and following two weeks of inactivity, it was officially closed from the 21st of the same month. Also on this date the L. N. E. R. closed Bow Road, whilst a year later a nearby blast slightly damaged its street level building and shattered the glass in the two London-end stairways. Previous to this, Bow Junction signal box received a direct hit in September 1940, and subsequently had to be totally rebuilt.

Goods depots of couse were also in the front line, and the first one to be affected was the old Midland establishment at Poplar Dock. This happened during the initial stages of the Blitz in September 1940, and resulted in its main warehouse being virtually flattened. Later that year, on the 29th of December, a similar fate befell both Royal Mint Street and Goodmans Yard, although here the outcome was less drastic, and the structures themselves received comparatively minor damage. Unfortunately however, Royal Mint Street was not destined to escape so lightly, and in the following Autumn it was hit again, and therefore had to be partially demolished. Around the same time this happened, a coal depot adjacent to the line at Cable Street became the scene of high drama when a bomb blew some loaded wagons off the track and caused one of them to hang from the viaduct, suspended only by its fragile coupling. At least one other fell into the street below, and the mess that ensued took many hours to clean up. Another depot that received bomb damage was Commercial Road, where the huge warehouse acquired a new flat roof in 1942, after suffering twice at the hands of the Nazis. During the height of the raids, its low level section provided refuge for thousands during the regular bombardments, and therefore the premises became known locally as 'The Tilbury Shelter'.

The early hours of May the 11th, 1941 saw a bomb fall on the north east end of Stepney East, which killed nearly forty people who were sheltering in one of the York Road arches beneath the railway. According to one of the survivors, it never actually exploded, and the victims died from falling masonry, but whether this is true or not is difficult to say. The arch itself was repaired by July but no-one could repair the heartbreak of those who lost their much loved relatives, nor could they bring back the innocents who died.

This incident occured on the night which was not only one of the worst of the Blitz, but also virtually the last. After this, the raids on East London moderated somewhat until the advent of the 'doodle-bugs', but by this time the damage had been done, and much of the area had been destroyed.

Leman Street and Shadwell stations, which had both been damaged in the bombing, were permanently closed from the 7th of July 1941, having managed to limp through the darkest months of the War. By this time, the surrounding district was so badly mauled by enemy action that it just wasn't worth keeping them open any longer.

In fact parts of the East End had changed out of all recognition during this period, and by the time that the hostilities finally drew to a close in 1945, many once familiar landmarks had disappeared forever. Amongst the losses from the local railway scene was the former North London route to Poplar, which bravely struggled on until the 15th of May 1944, when it finally succumbed to the inevitable. Poplar East India Road achieved the unenviable distinction of being the country's most frequently bombed station, and in the March of 1947 its pathetic remnants were finally taken down.

Shortly before this, the once proud, but now trackless Blackwall terminus fell to the demolition men, in order to provide a site for the new Brunswick power station. Had it survived a little longer it may have become the subject of a preservation order, but in the brave new post war Britain it didn't matter what buildings were sacrificed, as long as they were destroyed in the name of progress! Bit by bit this fine old structure fell to the ground, and within a few months one of London's oldest railway stations had disappeared completely. Nevertheless, as a sop to those who cared about such things at the time, the redevelopers thoughtfully retained the plaque which commemorated Captain John Smith, and transferred it to their new building. Perhaps this was an attempt to show that underneath their destructive exteriors they were really all heart, and that their intentions towards their country's heritage were entirely respectful. Personally I can't see why they even bothered, because although there are umpteen plaques around which bear little relevance to the cultural history of the East End, there was only one Blackwall station, and that regrettably no longer exists.

As far as the Blackwall Extension line was concerned, the late 'Forties brought the advent of electrification, although the preliminary work for this had been done a number of years earlier. In fact it owed its origins to a scheme which was announced by the L.N.E.R. on the 31st of December 1936, which outlined the modernisation of their suburban system as far as Shenfield, and also proposed to hand over the Ongar branch and Hainault Loop to London Transport.

Although a good deal of progress had been made on these projects, the War caused them to be temporarily abandoned, and therefore it wasn't possible for the work to be continued until 1946. Despite the fact that the plans for the L.N.E.R. were largely concerned with the ex-Great Eastern main line, they also envisaged electrification to Fenchurch Street, and for this reason, two bay platforms were provided at the rebuilt Stratford station. From here, a shuttle service was projected which would connect with the Liverpool Street trains and therefore retain the age old link which existed between the former Eastern Counties system and the old Blackwall Company's terminus. With this in mind, the L.N.E.R. reopened Bow Road station on the 9th of December 1946, but closed it again from the following 6th of January to allow improvements to be carried out.

They decided to give the place a face-lift, by shortening the awnings and fitting modern concrete lamp-posts, and once the work had been completed, it was brought back into commission from the 6th of October 1947. In fact their efforts made a great improvement to the station's appearance, and by allowing more light to reach the structure, they totally removed its former gloomy atmosphere. The canopies were retained around the tops of the London-end stairways, as well as the main platform buildings, but the rest were removed, and the sections of retaining wall which once supported them were reduced in height accordingly. To complement these modifications, the wooden fronted waiting rooms were given a new coat of green and cream paint, and this also helped to bring an element of cheer to the once dark and dingy station. Previously they had been bedecked in a finish of mid-brown and stone, which had been the standard colour scheme for L.N.E.R. lineside structures until about 1937. Very few, if any, of the other intermediate stations on the erstwhile Blackwall system received this new image until after the War, and it seems likely that Bow Road was the first one to be treated.

Unfortunately however, Bow Road's bright future wasn't to be, and after going through all the expense of modernisation and the installation of overhead catenaries, the decision was made that the line wasn't worth retaining, and therefore it had to close. By the time that this was publicised, the route had ceased to be owned by the L.N.E.R., as from the 1st of January 1948, it became part of the Eastern Region network belonging to the newly nationalised British Railways. The scheme for electrifying through to Fenchurch Street was abandoned because it was felt that it would largely duplicate existing bus and Underground routes, and therefore it didn't justify any further financial outlay. A closure date of the 7th of November 1949 was announced, and this was set to coincide with the introduction of through electric services between Liverpool Street and Shenfield. As there was no Sunday service, the last trains ran around lunchtime on Guy Fawke's Saturday. Once these had departed, the booking clerk locked his office at Bow Road for the last time, and the station was declared officially closed.

After operating for a complete century, the section of line between Gas Factory and Bow Junction was now totally bereft of its regular passenger traffic, and after being a mere guest at Fenchurch Street throughout its entire history, the former L. T. & S. R. system finally inherited a complete City terminus which it could now call its own.

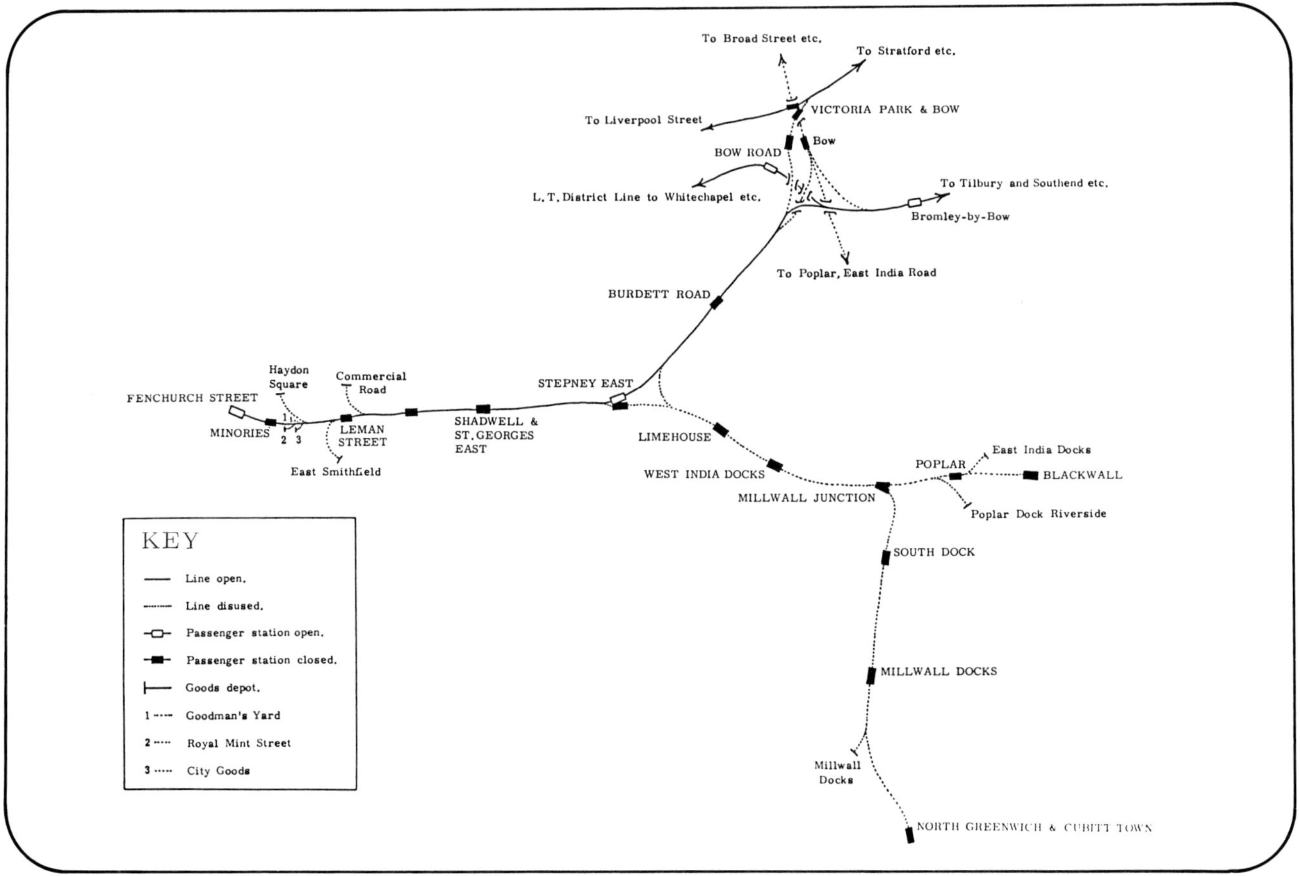

THE LONDON & BLACKWALL SYSTEM IN THE EARLY 1980's

THE WILDERNESS YEARS

Having used the costs of electrification as an excuse to cut the Bow Road services, British Railways then went ahead and wired the line up, stating that it would be a useful route to have in the event of an emergency. Once they had done this, they ran daily electrics over it, just for the purpose of keeping the wires clean. Whilst this was happening, Platforms 4 and 7 at Stratford, which were the two bays built for the line, waited in vain for the trains that never came, and the enamel directional signs in the subway beneath them had the deleted station names obliterated by a hasty coat of thick blue paint.

The 1500 volt dc overhead wires were erected along the complete length of the route, and ended above Platforms 1 and 2 at Fenchurch Street. To make room for the necessary catenaries, the disused stations at Burdett Road, Shadwell and Leman Street had their awnings removed, but other than this their surviving structures managed to linger on into the 1950's, when they were all finally demolished.

Apart from its canopies, Bow Road remained virtually intact until the October of 1967, when the old track-level buildings were eventually taken down. By this time they had become very tatty, but their basic shape was still there, and they continued to sport their faded coat of green and cream paintwork. The stairways at either end of the platforms were sealed off with breeze-blocks, but the pair leading to the exit still carried their attendant 'Way Out' signs. The structures also boasted two large boards which stated that 'Passengers Must Not Cross The Line', but the actual enamel plates which once displayed the station's name had presumably disappeared around the time it closed. The old covered way which once linked Bow Road with the adjoining North London establishment was taken over by a sweet manufacturer, and the long narrow passageway was converted into a factory. After closure, the former street-level building was leased to an electrical firm, whilst its predecessor on the opposite side of the main road was used as a shop. This structure, which is the only surviving remnant of the original 1876 station, has been used for many things since it closed, including a coal office and a tiny cinema, so naturally its appearance has changed considerably over the years. Although it still stands to the present day it now bears little resemblance to an old booking office, and it can be easily mistaken for something else. The later building however, is more easily identifiable, although since January 1982 it has been used as a betting office, and now has a rendered frontage. The doorway nearest the bridge has been converted into a window, and the whole thing now hides behind a coat of bright red paint. Nevertheless, a little of its character somehow continues to show through, and it's still certainly recognisable as a former station. Up on the viaduct, the two entrance stairways remain although the one on the east side has had its originally distinctive glass roof replaced by a more functional flat one. The platforms themselves are also still there, but they are now very overgrown and minus their coping. The stairways at the Stratford end were disused and semi-derelict even when the place was still open, but nevertheless they managed to survive until 1967, when they were demolished along with the old waiting room.

Other than Bow Road, there have been no further post-war passenger closures on the line, although all the goods depots have now gone. Most of these were damaged in the Blitz, and it therefore came as no surprise in the early 'Fifties when they began to be written off. The first to go was the old Midland Railway's City Goods Station on the 1st of July 1949, and this was followed two years later on the 1st of April 1951, by Goodman's Yard and Royal Mint Street. Poplar Dock, which had acquired the suffix 'Riverside' in January 1951 lingered on until the 4th of May 1956, although by this time it had been little used for some years. The others carried on for a bit longer, but during the cost-conscious 'Sixties, these too came under the axe. Not surprisingly, the next one to disappear was the old Great Northern depot at East India Dock, which closed around 1961. In later days it became a shadow of its former self, and the small amount of traffic that it continued to deal with was finally lost to road haulage. The remaining closures were all of establishments at the City end, and comprised Haydon Square, East Smithfield and Commercial Road. In many respects all of these had been 'white elephants', and perhaps they were lucky to survive as long as they actually did. Haydon Square had been opened by the London and North Western Railway in 1853, and for a little while it enjoyed a period of great prosperity. This importance however, was inclined to dwindle from 1868, when the same company constructed more convenient premises near Broad Street. Nevertheless it continued in use for another century, although by the time it closed on the 2nd of July 1962 its traffic had been whittled down to almost nothing. Of the other depots, East Smithfield had originally been planned as part of a larger complex which was intended to serve the London Docks. However, when it was found to be impossible to extend the tracks along the actual quayside, the scheme lost its impetus, and it finally settled down to a fairly mediocre existence. The main building at East Smithfield itself was extensively rebuilt by the L.N.E.R. in 1929, but as it never had the direct connection with the docks that originally had been hoped for, it failed to be used to its maximum capacity. In the end, the massive structure dealt with only a limited amount of traffic, and after a period of semi-disuse, it was finally taken out of commission from the 1st of September 1966. The final large depot to close was perhaps the biggest financial failure of them all, and this was the one at Commercial Road. Although it was an impressive building, the huge warehouse never really fulfilled the schemes of its promoters, and it's rather surprising that the establishment lasted as long as it did. The old 'guaranteed tonnage' agreement between the dock company and the L.T.& S.R was the cause of much trouble, and after many attempts at amending it,the idea was finally dropped in 1939. From this time onwards the P.L.A. paid a token rent for the premises, although by 1952, part of them were actually being used by the G.P.O. for parcel post. It was finally closed on the 3rd of July 1967, after which it was let to various tenants, and was also used as a car park. Its demolition commenced in the October of 1975, and the site of the main depot is now occupied by the National Westminster Bank's computer centre. Nevertheless parts of the branch which once served it are still in evidence, and the most noteworthy of these is a section of viaduct which leads alongside Pinchin Street, and terminates abruptly where it used to cross Backchurch Lane. Other than this, the depot's old hydraulic accumulator tower in Hooper Street still exists, and is in fact a Grade 2 listed building. On one of its walls can even be seen a poster board with the faded initials 'L.M.S.' still discernable at the top, and this, after so many years of nationalisation and disuse must be somewhat unusual.

The name of the same company is also still vaguely visible on the top of the old City Goods Station in Royal Mint Street. Although this structure is now derelict, it is nevertheless one of the last substantial relics of the many depots which once clustered around this section of the line, as Royal Mint Street G.N. and Goodmans Yard went many years ago. Admittedly there were a few scanty ruins of both of these at street level until fairly recently, but even these have now gone, and only the flimsiest remnants continue to exist. Underneath the railway bridge on the east side of the Minories, is an old doorway which a few people in the past have claimed as being part of the former passenger station.

The other establishment in the area, namely the short L.N.W.R. branch to Haydon Square, has also been virtually obliterated, although for many years after the main structure had been demolished, a large enamel sign continued to display its name above its entrance on the south side of Aldgate High Street.

This board was of the maroon, British Railways, London Midland Region type as the depot was managed by them during its last fourteen years. Apart from little off-shoots such as these however, the remainder of the former Blackwall system had become part of the Eastern Region after nationalisation, although for a short while the old L.T.& S.R. tracks east of Gas Factory Junction were allotted to the L.M.R. This changed from the 20th of February 1949, and although ex-L.M.S. engines continued to work the line, the routes to Tilbury, Southend and Shoeburyness officially came under the Eastern's banner.

In fact, the train services out of Fenchurch Street remained much the same between 1949 and the 6th of November 1961, when the first of the Southend electrics made their debut. For a few months these only ran outside the peak periods, but from the following 17th of June they took over the entire service, and the steam locomotives found themselves displaced.

By this time, the last of the old L.T.& S.R. type engines had been withdrawn, and the line was operated by a variety of 2-6-4 tanks. Of these, the original Stanier 3-cylinder machines were all taken out of commission, but the later L.M.S. and British Railways Standard locos were generally found work elsewhere.

Another innovation of this period was the addition of a new signalling panel at Fenchurch Street, which dispensed with the need of the old cabins at Stepney East and Gas Factory Junction. Once this was fully operational, the other boxes were closed, and both were later demolished.

The electrification was carried out to the new B.R. standard of 25kV and at the same time as this was installed, the old 1500 volts dc system from Stratford was changed accordingly.

Over the years, the link through Bow Road had proved its usefulness, although at the time of writing, it now lies rather derelict. Its first short period of glamour after closure came in the February of 1953, when the L.T.& S.R. line was cut by the disastrous Canvey Island floods, and no trains were able to pass between Benfleet and Leigh. For five days, special electrics were operated between Fenchurch Street and Shenfield, and from here, steam trains were available to take the commuters through to Southend. Another time that the link came into its own was on Saturday the 5th of December 1964, when a number of Shenfield line trains were re-routed into Fenchurch Street following a blaze which destroyed the Bishopsgate goods depot. This stood above the tracks, on the approaches to their normal terminus. Regular passengers looked a bit puzzled as their coaches squealed painfully round the sharp curve, and took them cautiously through the broken, gutted ruin that once was Bow Road. Sights like this had been fairly commonplace in the immediate post-war era, but by the mid-sixties, the existence of an intact, but abandoned station on a functional East London railway was somewhat of a rarity.

Apart from emergencies such as these, the line has been used for stock transference from the L.T.& S.R. route to Ilford Depot, and also for the odd enthusiast's special, but it has seen very little traffic for the past few years.

On the subject of enthusiast's specials, it was one of these that formed the final working over the Bow (North London) to Gas Factory Junction spur on the 21st of October 1967. This took the form of a diesel multiple unit, which operated from Fenchurch Street, and visited some of the lesser used routes of East London. Just two months after this, the steeply graded and historic line, which once provided access to the City for the infant 'Camden Town Railway' was officially closed, and in the months that followed, its tracks were subsequently removed.

Out of interest, the organisers of this trip, the Railway Correspondence and Travel Society, were also responsible, many years earlier, for chartering the last train to use the line between Stepney East and Limehouse Junction. This took place on the afternoon of Saturday the 14th of April 1951, and the special was formed of main line corridor stock, hauled by a former Great Eastern J69 class 0-6-0T No.E8619. It left the City at 2.30 pm then travelled direct to Millwall Junction, where it reversed and continued to North Woolwich, by way of the Limehouse Curve, Gas Factory Junction and Abbey Mills. After this it returned to Stepney, via the Bow Road line, and finally, after wandering around various junctions in the East Ham area, it eventually terminated at Stratford. The complete trip was scheduled to take 2 hours, 10 minutes, and the price of the ticket was as little as 3/6d. The participants of this tour were lucky indeed, for shortly after it had operated, the points were removed at Stepney East, and the original London & Blackwall main line west of Limehouse was down-graded to a siding. This continued to be reached from the eastern end, but it was only used occasionally for the delivery of scrap metal, and this was lifted by cranes into the adjoining premises, which belonged to George Cohen's 600 Group.

As mentioned earlier, the signal box at Stepney was removed after the Southend electrification came into being, and at the same time, the old 1849 signal tower which stood nearby was also demolished.

Beyond this, the old viaduct stretched along the side of the canal basin, still retaining part of its ornamental parapet, and even a few of the brackets which once supported its protective iron roof. As the years progressed, the rails were lifted, and eventually masses of buddleia bushes grew along the former trackbed. Despite this general air of dereliction however, the historical significance of the structure was fortunately not forgotten, and because of this it was granted a preservation order.

Another item of interest, although unrelated to the line, is the strange castle-like octagonal tower, with a truncated chimney, which stands between the diverging viaducts at Limehouse Junction. This has sometimes been mistaken for a railway structure in the past, but it is in fact London's oldest surviving accumulator tower, and it was built for the Regents Canal Dock in 1852. It is now a Grade 2 listed structure, and the Ragged School Museum Trust have plans to utilise it as part of an 'interpretation centre' for local railway and canal history.

The Limehouse Curve itself was taken out of use on the 5th of November, 1962, and it was disconnected from the passenger route on the following 10th of May. Eleven chains east of Limehouse Junction was the centre of the old passenger station platforms, although all trace of these disappeared about 1929. Now their site is only marked by a partial widening of the viaduct, where the stairwells once were, although down at street level, the former entrance in Three Colt Street remains more or less intact.

Unfortunately the same thing cannot be said of West India Docks, which was situated another twenty-five chains further on, and stood on the east side of the road with the same name. Here the entire station was demolished between 1931 and 1934, and today not the slightest traces remain of it.

In Trinidad Street, on the south side of the viaduct between the sites of West India Docks and Limehouse stations were the frontages of four houses, which were built within two of the arches when the line was first constructed. These were converted for storage purposes many years ago, but until very recently their interiors still exhibited traces of what they once were.

To the east of the bridge that crosses the West India Dock Road could be seen the site of the old Midland coal depot on the down side of the line. This was closed on the 6th of November 1967, and as it was reached from the former North London system, it managed to outlive the old Blackwall tracks by about one year.

Beyond here, the line was brought down from the viaduct on an earth embankment, until it reached the remains of Millwall Junction. On the down side, between the two stations, once stood the signal box, where heavily laden freight trains often had to wait for banking assistance to help them with the climb towards central London. Latterly all that could be seen was wasteland, although to the north, the rusty rails of the old Harrow Lane marshalling yard still stared defiantly through the ever increasing amount of undergrowth.

At Millwall Junction, the old platforms remained in situ until around 1985, although for some years they were virtually hidden by weeds. The building which once stood between the up main and diverging branch was removed some twenty years earlier, although the footbridge which formerly connected it with the outside world survived for about another decade. Beyond here, the cutting that led towards Blackwall was filled in during the 1970's and so little is now visible. Until the late 'Sixties, a fair bit still remained at Poplar, but all this has now disappeared. At the junction with the Midland Dock branch, the pathetic vandalised remains of the signal box were mercifully removed around 1964, although the intriguing red brick building, which was mentioned in the last chapter, managed to survive another five years or so. Although no trace of any equipment remained inside its bare empty shell, it seems likely that this structure could well have housed the hydraulic equipment necessary for the operation of the depot's capstans, and its similarity with the nearby pump house help to bear this out. It's a shame that such an interesting building had to be pulled down, but for the time being at least the main pump house is still standing, and for admirers of the Midland Railway style of architecture this is a real gem.

On the opposite side of Brunswick Street, or Blackwall Way as it is now called both the dock branch and main line have been virtually obliterated, although part of the Midland depot wall has survived together with a few small buildings. North of these can be seen an imposing three storey house, which dates from the mid 19th Century, and was built for the Green family who owned the nearby shipbuilding yards. This is constructed of brick with stucco embellishments, and is currently used as offices for the Blackwall Engineering Company.

Adjoining this building's north wall, the top of the brick lined cutting which once accommodated Poplar Station can still be seen, although the cutting itself has been filled in to road level. Near the site of the former entrance, a section of wall remains with some painted plaster, and handrail brackets clearly indicate the course of the up side stairway. Until the late 'Sixties this was a good vantage point to view the long empty station platforms, which still looked much the same as they had since their awnings were removed. Despite their apparent desolation there were still a few interesting items to be found, including an old Great Eastern signal at the west end of the up platform. This was still fitted with both its 'home' and its 'distant' arms, and although these were made of wood, they seemed to be well preserved. Most of the actual buildings had gone in the 1930s, so the only structures that remained were the former lamp room, which once sat beneath the down side stairway, and the gents toilet which stood at the opposite end of the other platform. Other than these, there was little of note, although on a good day, when the sun was in the right position, it was just about possible to make out the line of the former up-side canopy on the brickwork of the southern retaining wall.

From the east end of the station could be seen the battered wooden hulk of Brunswick Junction signal box, which had lost its true purpose with the closure of the East India Dock freight branch in 1961. It nevertheless continued to function a little longer, and in its last days, it witnessed the sight of a few forlorn steam locomotives being towed to a scrapyard which had set up business on the former depot site. Probably the most noteworthy of these was the little 'Y4' type 0-4-0T, which once shunted around the railway works at Stratford, but there was also J15 0-6-0 No.65445, and a B1 4-6-0 as well. In a nearby yard which was reached from the former North London line, BEL No. 1 the four-wheeled battery shunter from West India Docks, was also consigned to the scrap heap around the same time, although it was stored for a while beneath a tarpaulin sheet before it was finally broken up.

After Brunswick Junction the tracks had been taken up, and the former earthworks only continued for a short distance before they came to an abrupt halt at the wall of the Blackwall Power Station. Unfortunately however, even all this has now gone.

On the North Greenwich branch, the only remaining substantial relic is the narrow viaduct which straddles across Millwall Park. Other than this, the little terminus survived as a sailing club until 1969, but it then became dangerous, so it was replaced by a new purpose built structure. In its final days it was very decrepit, and the warped and crumbling woodwork was inclined to conjure up visions of a derelict ghost town, somewhere in the mid-west of America.

As the stations at Millwall Docks and South Dock had both long gone, the only other surviving item of interest on the line was the old Saxby & Farmer signal cabin near Millwall Junction. This stood in all its flaking glory until fairly recently, but it has now been demolished. Close to this, but on the railway rather than the dock side of the boundary fence, once lay an ancient coach body which for years had been used as a staff mess room. This survived well into the 1970s, but with the combined forces of vandalism and the weather, the whole thing eventually collapsed, and its remains were presumably carted away.

As far as stations on the surviving British Rail section of the line are concerned, Stepney East is of course still very much in the land of the living. It was officially renamed Limehouse on Monday the 11th of May 1987, although the nameboards were actually altered a few days earlier. The old Blackwall line platforms disappeared many years ago and until recent developments, all that could be said to remain of them was the flat area which marked the spot where the up-side stairwell once surfaced. The Tilbury and Southend part of the station however is delightful, and well worth inspection. At the City end of the down platform there is a section of awning which is certainly earlier than the rest, and probably pre-dates its 1876 rebuilding. This is supported by wooden uprights, and its general styling suggests the 1850s period. Further along this side, adjacent to a now disused entrance, can be found a small stone drinking fountain presented by the St. George's Tufnell Park Band of Mercy. This is a relic of the days when a few 'better off' Londoners believed that kindness towards the underpriviliged East Enders would help to buy their souls a first class ticket to heaven, and therefore went around looking for trivial 'good works' into which they could throw their surplus finances. All this aside however, the little fountain is not unattractive, and its survival after so many years on an inner suburban railway station must be fairly unusual. The nearby abandoned entrance was reached through a doorway on the north side of Commercial Road, and has been long out of use. Life returned briefly however a few years ago, when the main stairway was being rebuilt, and a temporary replacement had to be found. A hastily painted nameboard was placed on the wall at street-level, and the old stairs were brought back into commission, but a fire broke out, and after a very short period, the whole thing was shut up again.

On the up platform, the main building appears to date from the early 1890s, as it is very similar to the erstwhile structures at Bow Road. Other than some fairly minor alterations, this seems to be still as built, and one of its windows continues to display the title 'General Waiting Room' in etched lettering. The majority of canopy valancing on this side is also of Great Eastern origin, although its counterpart across the tracks has unfortunately been altered.

At street level, the booking hall was a pure delight, with a small passimeter office, which came complete with a nice blue glass 'Way In' sign and beneath this a window with 'Please Show Tickets' in gilded print. This structure was removed around 1986, when it was replaced by a new office, and consequently a great deal of character has been lost. As far as the actual entrances were concerned, they were simply large, arched doorways set within the viaduct itself, and in no way could they claim to have any architectural detailing.

The same thing however cannot be said of the two war-damaged closed stations that can be found west of Stepney, as both of these had quite substantial street level buildings.

Shadwell & St. Georges East had its entrance on the west side of Sutton Street, and this still exists in its entirety. It adjoins the south side of the viaduct, and probably dates from its 1895 - 1896 rebuilding. Its general appearance is similar to the corresponding structure at Limehouse, although it is built of red brick instead of grey. Unfortunately everything at track level was demolished in 1956, although a fragment of platform still exists on the up side to block up the hole that was vacated by the stairwell.

Heading towards Fenchurch Street, the line passes the site of the short-lived establishment at Cannon Street Road, but this was demolished in the last century, and nothing remains whatsoever.

Until recently, Leman Street possessed can be found what was probably the most substantial station remains on the line, other than those at Bow Road.

Here the up platform survived, tatty and minus its coping stones, but otherwise basically intact. Its buildings disappeared at the same time as those at Shadwell, but the stairwell remained, and had some nice decorative ironwork along the edge parallel to the track. The stairs themselves had gone, although a few shattered remnants remained at the top. Their course down to the booking hall however was clearly visible, and prominent traces of old brown and cream painted plaster clung hopefully to the adjoining walls. Inside the old booking hall there was nothing but gutted devastation, and a colony of pigeons, but the exterior was still recognisable as what it once was. There were two entrances, one on the corner of Leman Street and Cable Street, and another facing Backchurch Lane. Of these, the former, which of course was the main one, still retained a large iron lamp bracket above its doorway, but this disappeared a few years ago. Other than the up platform already described, there was nothing left at track-level, although the truncated remains of the London Docks branch could be seen at the west end. Latterly there were a couple of bids to turn the old booking hall into commercial premises, but these were both unsuccessful, and until its final demise, it remained derelict, with its doorways and windows sealed up. The whole thing was swept away to facilitate the construction of the Docklands Light Railway, and now only scanty signs remain to indicate where it once stood.

The only other closed station as yet unmentioned is Burdett Road, where everything alongside the line has long-since been swept away. The former entrance was situated on the north-east side of the road, and was hidden away in almost subterranean gloom of a narrow pedestrian archway.The former booking hall was used as a factory until recent times, but it later became derelict. The northernmost door was a modern replacement, but the other one was original, and had some characteristic panelling, similar to that at Stepney East. Apart from the windows adjacent to the entrance, there were also similar openings either side of the viaduct, but these appeared to have been bricked-up for many years, and were probably out of use by the time the station closed. The section of viaduct wall that included the former street-level accommodation was picked out with a degree of decorative stone work, and some of this displayed the scars of the Second World War up to the time of its demolition. The surviving remains disappeared around 1984 when the overbridge was renewed, and now only a widening of the viaduct at track level indicates its former site.

North-east of here, the Southend line electrics speed past Gas Factory Junction, and head towards their next stop at Barking or Upminster. Few of their passengers realise that part of the line which they have just travelled over is one of the oldest railways in London, and an equally small number are probably aware of the existence of the now closed stations. In their day they were an integral part of the lives of so many East Enders, but as time marches on, they are slipping further into obscurity. I hope that these few chapters have helped record them before they become finally forgotten, and that reading about the line's fascinating past has stirred both memories and imagination.

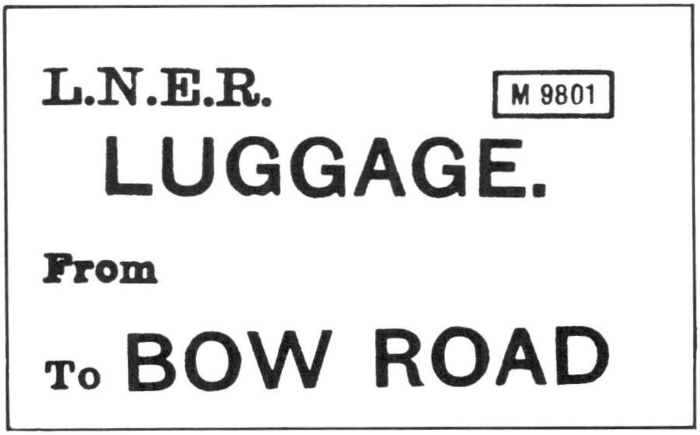
L.N.E.R. M 9801
LUGGAGE.
From
To BOW ROAD

A LONDON & NORTH EASTERN RAILWAY LUGGAGE LABEL

THE PHOENIX AWAKES

In 1981, the Central Government announced plans which they hoped would bring back life to around eight square miles of semi-derelict wasteland, and they set up an organisation which they called the London Docklands Development Corporation. The aim of this body was to tempt commercial development into the area, and by allowing unrestrictive planning permission to prospective businesses, they intended to complete this task within ten to fifteen years. To encourage this redevelopment, they proposed a new rapid transit system, which would utilise a great deal of the disused London & Blackwall formation, and this received formal government approval in December 1982. The scheme was to be known as the Docklands Light Railway, and the cost of construction was estimated at £77 million. The L.D.D.C. offered to contribute 50% of this, whilst the Greater London Council agreed to supply the remainder.

The new system was initially projected to extend from a City station at the Minories through to Island Gardens, Millwall, with a branch line from Poplar to Mile End. This section however was to prove rather impractical as it involved constructing a street tramway between Bow and the proposed terminus, and therefore the scheme was later modified. For a while the local press made scathing comments, and said that the area needed a railway which was fully integrated with the existing London Transport system. However, the promoters claimed that this would be ruled out by costs, and that an extension from the Minories to Aldgate East would entail a minimum additional outlay of £10 million.

Meanwhile, the job of redeveloping the derelict dock estates of the Isle of Dogs was gathering momentum, and a new urban landscape began to take on a recognisable shape. The docks themselves had been in a sad decline for some years, and by this time all commercial activity within them had completely ceased. A large Asda store was constructed at Crossharbour, and nearby a sports complex was planned, capable of accommodating 12,000 people. All this activity was fitting in nicely with the regeneration scheme for the area, and the L.D.D.C. stated that when completed, their efforts would hopefully create around 9,000 new jobs.

The first Bill for the construction of the Docklands Light Railway was deposited in the November of 1982, and received the Royal

Assent in April 1984. This only authorised the section between the Minories and the Isle of Dogs, but a second Bill, introduced in November 1983 and passed in April 1985, gave the go-ahead for the route north of Poplar. This was to proceed as initially planned, and utilise the former N.L.R. trackbed as far as Bow, but instead of running along the street to Mile End, the promoters agreed that it would be better to operate into Stratford. This would of course alleviate any disruption that the service might have suffered due to road congestion, and also afford a better connection with British Rail and London Regional Transport. Another advantage of this scheme was that the D.L.R. could make use of an existing trackbed and also a ready-made bay platform at Stratford station.

The new system was to be known as a 'Light Railway', not because it was to be constructed under a Light Railway Order, but because it was to benefit from the latest technology associated with 'Light Rail Transit'. This form of transportation is neither conventional railway nor tramway, but embodies certain features from both. Its versatility, particularly in urban areas, has proved highly commendable, and in addition to finding success on the Continent and in America, it is also used for the Tyne and Wear Metro around Newcastle and Gateshead.

The initial stages of construction began in 1984, and one of the first jobs was the clearing of weeds and bushes from the former Blackwall viaduct east of Stepney. G.E.C./Mowlem were appointed as contractors, and a deadline of Summer 1987 was set for completion. The building work proceeded with impressive speed, and within a year parts of the railway were beginning to take shape.

At the City end, an imposing terminus began to materialise at the Minories, whilst the existing viaduct between there and Cannon Street Road was widened on its south side by the addition of a steel and concrete extension. The construction of this necessitated the demolition of Leman Street station, and now little is left to indicate where it once stood. However, some of the lower brick courses of the up platform have survived, and these have been used to partially support the new D.L.R. trackbed.

By 1986, the scheme was well under way, and track had been laid along much of the route. This work was sub-contracted by the Scunthorpe firm of Grant Lyon Eagre Ltd., and their little four wheel diesel engines hauling engineers trains became the first motive power to operate over the system. The majority of rails used were of the light 80 lb type, but the section between Cannon Street Road and Stepney, where former British Rail tracks were employed, retained the existing 113 lb flat bottom rails.

As only eleven trains would be required to operate the initial service, it was deemed uneconomical to pay a British firm to tool up for them, and therefore an order was placed with Linke Hoffman Busch in Salzgitter, West Germany. This company already possessed the necessary jigs and production line facilities, and this of course helped to keep down the cost of their construction.

The units each consist of two coaches, connected by an articulated joint, and are constructed of a steel framework with external steel cladding panels. They have a total length of 91' 10" (28m), and weigh 38.4 tons (39 tonnes). They have a seating capacity of eighty-four passengers, with sufficient space for a hundred and thirty standing, and they are capable of operating at a maximum speed of 80 kilometres per hour. Although their basic bodywork comes from Germany, their control and traction equipment has been designed by G.E.C., and some of their other details, such as the traditional moquette covered seats, are also British. The trains work automatically without a driver, and their electro-pneumatic inward gliding doors have press buttons to allow passengers to open them as required.

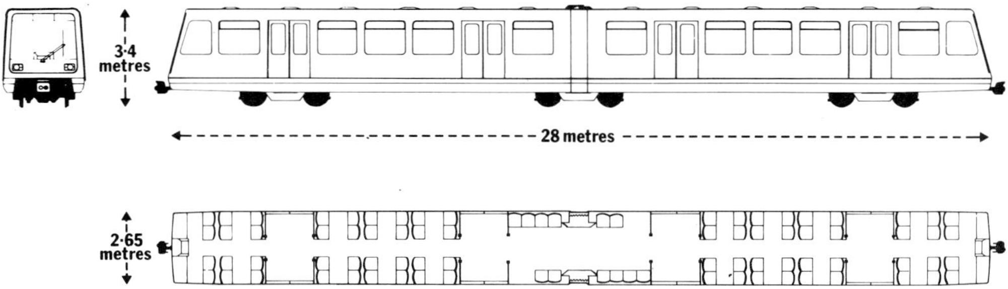

D.L.R. UNIT SHOWING BASIC LAYOUT AND DIMENSIONS
Docklands Light Railway Ltd.

Work on the first unit commenced at Salzgitter early in 1986, and later that year, on the 8th of August, it was delivered to the railway's Operations and Maintenance Centre at Poplar. It created a very favourable impression with the press, and its striking red white and blue paint scheme set off its modernistic lines perfectly.

As 1987 dawned, the system appeared to be more or less complete, with only comparatively small tasks still to be overcome. The majority of the engineering work had been finished, and the long derelict remains of 'Stepney's Own Railway' were being prepared for their reincarnation.

The stations along the line are all constructed from standard components, and therefore have the same basic appearance. The concrete platforms are 98'6" (30m) long, and these are protected by 29'6" (9m) glass and iron canopies. They each have stairway access from the street but this is supplemented by hydraulic lifts which have been installed for the convenience of those who are disabled, or over-loaded with shopping. All the premises are totally unstaffed, and therefore passengers must obtain their tickets from the machines that are positioned near the station entrances. The equipment for these has been provided by Thorn-EMI, and the tickets themselves are of thin card with an oxide strip on the back. When these are placed in an adjoining machine they become validated, and are therefore made good for travel.

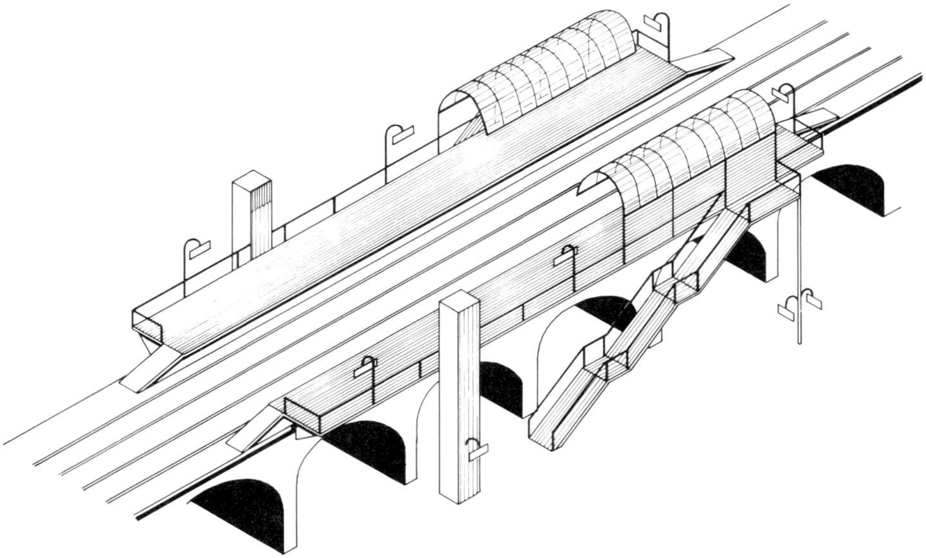

ARCHITECT'S ILLUSTRATION OF AN ELEVATED D.L.R. STATION.

Docklands Light Railway Ltd.

Various stations were renamed prior to opening, and amongst these was the City terminus. Originally this was to have been called Minories, but this was changed firstly to Tower Hill and later to Tower Gateway. This is an impressive structure with a glass domed entrance leading onto glass covered stairways, and it adjoins the site of the old Minories station of 1840. At track level, there is a single island platform fed by a spacious circulating area, and the impression created is attractive and tasteful.

The D.L.R. is taken from this terminus on a new structure which continues alongside the Blackwall viaduct as far as Cannon Street Road, but after this it utilises the two former slow lines on the south side of the earlier formation. The first intermediate station is situated at Shadwell, where a simple island affair has been positioned at the west end of the original site. Looking eastwards from here, it is still possible to see a short remnant of disused platform beside the line, and this marks the spot where the stairs once surfaced from the old booking office in Sutton Street.

The route continues along erstwhile British Rail metals until a little west of Stepney, where a 200 metre section of reinforced concrete viaduct has been constructed to allow a better clearance of existing tracks. As mentioned in the last chapter, Stepney East station has now been renamed Limehouse, which although technically accurate, may prove a little confusing for those who are familiar with it. The British Rail booking hall is now reached through a new doorway in Bekesbourne Street, adjoining the D.L.R. premises, and the former entrance on the south side of Commercial Road has been bricked up. At the time of writing, the pair of doors beneath the railway bridge to the east of this old entrance remain untouched, and these are surmounted by a nice Victorian iron lamp-bracket. These doors once served an additional exit from the Up Bow line platform, and although this has long since been sealed up at track level, the crumbling wooden stairway remains, complete with a ticket gate on the ground floor.

The D.L.R. station at Limehouse consists of two standard side platforms and these occupy the site of the former Stepney East Blackwall line structures that were demolished in the 1930s.

Beyond Limehouse the D.L.R. utilises the old viaduct beside the Regent's Canal Basin, and this has had its ornamental cast iron balustrading nicely renovated. After so many years of disuse and decay, it's good to see this fine old structure again serving a useful purpose, although unfortunately some of the necessary re-pointing has given it rather a patchy appearance in places. Some other sections of viaduct have been topped by reproduction London & Blackwall style railings, which although very attractive when viewed from the street, are marred a little by having open-backed stanchions instead of the solid variety as originally fitted. This is nevertheless a nice gesture, and at least it shows that the new management have respect for their railway's past.

At the former Limehouse Junction, the sixty-foot high hydraulic accumulator tower still stands sentinel beside the line, whilst a little further east, the site of the old Limehouse station remains much as it has since the platforms were demolished nearly sixty years ago.

The next D.L.R. station is named Westferry, and is situated west of the former West India Docks station of the L. & B.R. It straddles both Limehouse Causeway and Westferry Road, and comprises of two platforms built to the standard design.

Beyond here, the line crosses West India Dock Road, then climbs away from the old viaduct on a sharp gradient to a high level junction known as North Quay. Here the system is carried on a totally new network of concrete structures, and is close to the Operations & Maintenance Centre. This is the hub of the new railway, where Controllers keep an eye on the day to day running, and are in closed-circuit television contact with all the stations. This large building also houses the D.L.R.'s repair shops, and stands to the south of Poplar High Street, near the site of the old Harrow Lane sidings.

From North Quay Junction, the route to Island Gardens heads southwards and passes through the stations at West India Quay, Canary Wharf, Heron Quays, South Quay and Crossharbour before joining the old Millwall Extension Railway. This new section of the route is partially carried on a series of bridges over the former West India group of docks, and these give passengers excellent views of the surrounding area.

Although the line south of Crossharbour is built on the erstwhile North Greenwich branch trackbed, a new bridge has had to be installed over East Ferry Road to replace the one that was demolished in 1937, and this supports the next D.L.R. station which has the somewhat curious sounding name of 'Mudchute'. This title owes its origins to a pneumatic dredger that was developed in the 1880's to overcome gradual silting up of the nearby dock, and it was chosen instead of the previously intended name of 'Millwall Park'. Its entrance is situated on the east side of East Ferry Road, and is sited to the south of the long-since vanished Millwall Docks station.

Beyond Mudchute the two tracks join into one, and are carried on the old single-line North Greenwich branch viaduct across Millwall Park. A new bridge has been installed over Manchester Road, and immediately after this, the route comes to an end at Island Gardens.

The new terminus is situated at the City end of the old North

Greenwich station site, and is provided with two platforms that splay out in a 'vee' formation. Between these, at street level, is positioned the ticket concourse and this has a domed roof that has been built to resemble the similar structure on the nearby foot tunnel entrance. The original short section of viaduct south of Manchester Road was unsuitable to support the new premises, and therefore had to be replaced. The present structure consists of concrete arches, and these have been clad with bricks to match the appearance of the main viaduct.

The Poplar to Stratford section diverges at North Quay, and passes the new Billingsgate Fish Market before joining the former N.L.R. route to Dalston. Nearby lies the site of Millwall Junction, but this has now almost disappeared, and little remains to indicate where it once stood except around 80 ft of retaining wall which stands to the east of the curve, alongside the Docklands Northern Relief Road.

The D.L.R. continues northwards, and uses the old alignment as far as the scanty remnants of Bow (NL) station. Here the double track formation comes to an end, and the permanent way becomes single. At Bow, a steeply graded curving embankment has been built to enable the trains to reach the level of the Great Eastern main line, and after running parallel to this for a short distance, they terminate alongside Platform Four at Stratford. This is one of the bays constructed for the abortive Fenchurch Street shuttle service of the 1940s, and until the advent of the D.L.R., it has never been used.

Leading up to the opening, the D.L.R. operated numerous trial trips, and it was a strange sight to see a totally empty unit, without even a driver, pull up at an equally deserted station. The event was made even more eerie by the presence of a taped announcement calling out the train's destination over the speaker system. Of course everything went to plan, although on the evening of Tuesday the 10th of March 1987, a train overshot Island Gardens, and ended up precariously hanging over the top of the viaduct. This however, was only a minor hiccup, and the method by which the line is operated is now proving to be more successful.

Although coming under the banner of London Regional Transport, the Docklands Light Railway has its own identity and livery: The prominent house colour is blue, and this appears on everything from stations to the uniforms of the 'Train Captains'. These are members of staff who travel on the services to ensure that all is well, and also check passengers' tickets. The trains themselves are painted in a medium shade of blue, with red applied in a horizontal sash below the windows, and vertically over the doors. The lining between these two colours is carried out with broad bands of white, and the legend 'Docklands' appears either side of each unit.

The trains operate from a power supply of 750v dc, and current is collected from a bottom contact conductor rail. This has a plastic shroud protecting the top and sides, and is less prone to problems in icy weather conditions than traditional track level pick-ups. The units are fitted with copper shoes on glass reinforced plastic arms and these are mounted in a central position, either side of the motor bogies.

With the line now complete, all appeared to be ready for the opening in July 1987.

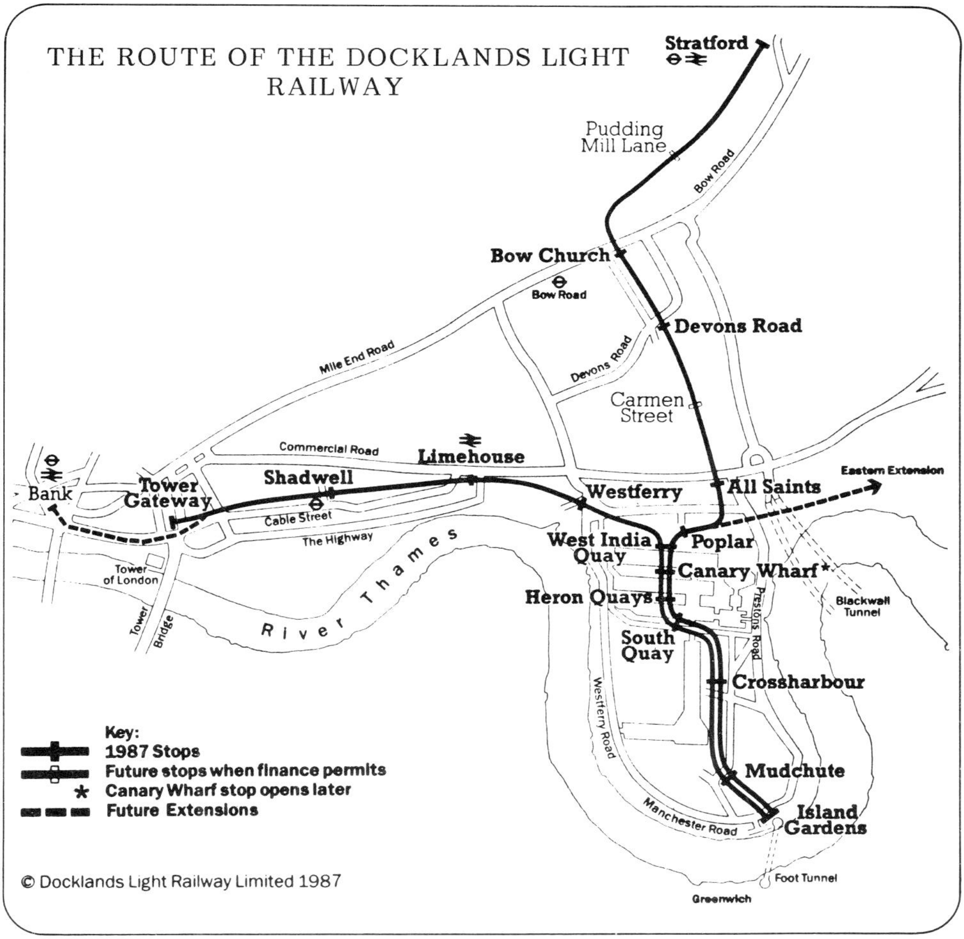

THE ROUTE OF THE DOCKLANDS LIGHT RAILWAY

DAWN OF A NEW ERA

In the weeks leading up to the proposed opening date, it became apparent to the operating authorities, that the units were still suffering from minor teething troubles, and therefore a little extra time would be beneficial before the commencement of the full public service. With this in mind the D.L.R. announced that the inauguration would have to be postponed for a while, although the Royal opening would proceed as planned on Thursday the 30th of July. This meant that the line would be declared 'open' and then technically 'Closed' immediately afterwards to allow the various problems to be resolved.

At around ten past three on the afternoon of July 30th, Her Majesty the Queen, accompanied by the Duke of Edinburgh, disembarked from the PLA launch 'Royal Nore' near Island Gardens, and was escorted to the station by the Mayor of Tower Hamlets, and the Chairman of the LDDC. Here she met Sir Keith Bright, the Chairman of LRT, and was invited to unveil a commemorative plaque. Following this, the Royal Artillery Band played the National Anthem, and the Queen formally opened the railway.

After inspecting the operation of the ticket machines and validators, the Royal Party boarded their train at Platform 2, and travelled to South Quay, where they visited the nearby Daily Telegraph building. They later journeyed to Poplar for a reception at the Operations and Maintenance Centre, and then continued to Tower Gateway, where they were escorted down the escalator to cars that were waiting in the street below.

The Royal Train was suitably bedecked with a special headboard, and parties of local school children were allowed on the platforms at Mudchute, Crossharbour, Westferry and Limehouse to watch it pass by.

In the weeks that followed it became apparent that everything was functioning correctly, and therefore a press release was issued on the 24th of August stating that the passenger service would begin on the following Bank Holiday Monday.

By 05.00 on the 31st of August, Poplar station began to buzz with activity, as crowds of enthusiastic passengers, accompanied by representatives of the news media waited the arrival of the stock for the first train. There was a short speech by Mr. Cliff Bonnett, the Managing Director of the D.L.R., welcoming everyone to the new railway, and then, at around 05.15, unit No.01 appeared out of the darkness, and pulled up at the platform.

For the first time, the general public could view the system at close quarters, and see the Train Captains in their smart blue uniforms, which were specially adorned for the event by red carnation button-holes.

After everyone had taken their quota of photographs, they were ushered on board by the Train Captains, and a minute or so later than the booked 05.17, the little train set off on its journey to Island Gardens. Despite the early hour, the unit was full and standing, and all the passengers who had forsaken a few hours of extra sleep were rewarded with a commemorative medallion, that was handed to them by the D.L.R. Publicity Officer. The train sped through the dark, calling briefly at the closely spaced stations, and within ten minutes it arrived at Island Gardens.

After a short wait, the unit departed, and travelled to Stratford, where it again reversed, and returned to the Isle of Dogs.

During these trips, Mr. Cliff Bonnett travelled on the train, and happily autographed various souvenir items such as tickets and philatelic covers. In fact, a bright cheerful atmosphere prevailed throughout the day, helped in no small way by the enthusiasm of the staff, and the friendliness of the Train Captains in particular.

By 06.00 the sun was beginning to rise, and a mellow pink sky heralded the dawn of a new chapter in London's railway history.

Apart from a slight lull between the hours of six and eleven in the morning, the trains ran to capacity, and when the first day of public service was over, the D.L.R. had carried around 50,000 passengers.

At the time of writing all of the D.L.R. stations are in use, with the exception of Canary Wharf, where construction has been delayed whilst plans for the adjoining financial complex are being finalised. Work on this station was virtually complete, and needed only ticket facilities and nameboards to make it ready for opening. However, the decision was made to rebuild it on a much larger scale, and therefore it was dismantled during August 1987. All re-usable parts have been put into store, and will be brought out again if needed for another station. The much enlarged structure will open at a later date, but until then trains will stop at the site as they are programmed to do so.

Passenger services on the D.L.R. operate from Island Gardens to either Tower Gateway or Stratford, and for ease of public identification, these have been designated as 'Green' and 'Red' routes respectively. These colours are clearly indicated on the system's diagrammatic maps, and are also used as a background on train destination boards or screens.

Services normally operate on Mondays to Fridays between 05.17 and around 00.30, whilst on Sunday they run between 07.17, and around 23.30. The frequency varies according to the time of day, but basically, each line has a train approximately every ten to twelve minutes. The section between West India Quay and Island Gardens is served by both 'Green' and 'Red' routes, and therefore has a more intensive service.

Although it is technically possible to operate directly between Tower Gateway and Stratford, by means of the northern side of the triangular North Quay Junction, this is not normally done. However, a few trains around the start and finish of traffic each day do in fact run over these tracks as they require to travel from and to the depot at Poplar. Passengers intending to make a journey that involves both 'Green' and 'Red' routes are advised to take a train to West India Quay, and then change.

A complete journey along the full length of the 'Green' route is booked to take 16 minutes, whilst a similar ride on the 'Red' line should take two minutes longer. Either way, the Docklands Light Railway provides an excellent means of getting around part of London that was previously long-since devoid of trains, and a trip along its metals is a unique and enjoyable experience.

Having successfully opened the bulk of the system, the D.L.R. has plans for an extension between Tower Gateway and the Bank, and this will probably materialise in the not too distant future.

After descending from the viaduct a little east of the Minories, the new line will enter a tunnel, and proceed for a distance of 1.5km to a spacious terminus beneath King William Street. The extension is being sponsored by a consortium of three Investment Banks who are planning an international finance centre at Canary Wharf, and they claim that its existence is an essential part of their scheme. The development is expected to comprise of three high rise towers, together with around 10 million square feet of office accommodation, and it has been nick-named 'Wall Street on the Water'.

An eastern extension of the D.L.R. between Poplar and Beckton is also a possibility, but so far this is only at the preliminary stages of planning, and it will be some time before it comes into fruition.

It has been claimed by the D.L.R. management that the railway will earn its place in the record books for the speed in which is has been developed, and they are probably right. Their system is no doubt the most revolutionary line that London has seen for many years, and all involved in its construction have a good reason to feel satisfied.

After nearly 150 years, it seems that the wheel of fate has turned full circle, and the historic route between the City and Poplar is again host to a totally unconventional railway. For lovers of the steam age, the D.L.R. may look uncompromisingly modern, but no doubt if fast automatic electric trains had been around in 1840, the original promoters of the London & Blackwall system would have given them their full approval!

Docklands Light Railway tickets
issued on the first day of public service:
The specimen from Shadwell was dated 1904 in error!

Appendix One

CHRONOLOGY OF MAIN EVENTS

1836 (8th Feb.) - Initial section of London & Greenwich Railway opened to the public. (THIS WAS THE FIRST ORTHODOX RAILWAY LINE IN LONDON.)

1839 (20th June) - Initial section of Eastern Counties Railway opened to the public between Devonshire Street and Romford. Track gauge was non-standard 5'.

1840 (6th July) - LONDON AND BLACKWALL RAILWAY OPENED TO THE PUBLIC, using rope traction, and non-standard track gauge of 5'.

1841 (2nd Aug.) - L. & B. line extended westwards from the Minories to a new terminus at Fenchurch Street. THIS WAS THE FIRST STATION TO BE BUILT WITHIN THE ACTUAL CITY OF LONDON.

1844 (5th Sept. - 7th Oct.) - Track gauge of Eastern Counties Railway converted to standard 4' 8½".

1849 (14th Feb.) - Last day of rope haulage and 5' track gauge on London & Blackwall Railway. Also, Blackwall Extension Railway opened for freight traffic between Stepney Junction and Bow Common Junction.

1849 (2nd April) - Blackwall Extension Railway opened for passengers.

1850 (26th Sept.) - Initial section of East & West India Docks and Birmingham Junction Railway opened, with passenger service between Islington and Fenchurch Street.

1853 (1st Jan.) - East & West India Docks and Birmingham Junction Railway changed its name to the North London Railway.

1854 (13th April) - Initial section of London, Tilbury & Southend Railway opened between Forest Gate Junction and Tilbury Fort. Passenger trains operated into both Fenchurch Street (L. & B.) and Shoreditch (E.C.R.)

1856 - London & Blackwall viaduct between Fenchurch Street and Stepney widened, and provided with additional Up line.

1862 (7th Aug.) - Royal Assent given to Bill which incorporated Eastern Counties system as part of the new Great Eastern Railway.

1865 (1st Nov.) - North London Railway opened their 'Happy Afterthought' line between Dalston and Broad Street.

1866 (1st Jan.) - London & Blackwall Railway leased to the Great Eastern Railway for 999 years.

1869 (1st Jan.) - Great Eastern Railway took over the working of the Fenchurch Street - Bow trains from the North London Railway. After this N.L.R. trains ceased to use Fenchurch Street.

1870 (1st Sept.) - North London Railway trains extended from Poplar, East India Road station into Blackwall, mainly in connection with river traffic from Brunswick Pier.

1871 (18th Dec.) - Millwall Extension Railway opened for workmen between Millwall Junction and Millwall Docks station. Single coach 'train' was hauled by two horses to avoid fire risks on dock property.

1872 (29th July) - M.E.R. extended from Millwall Docks to North Greenwich & Cubitt Town. Steam traction used in isolation between the boundary of the Millwall Dock Company's property and the branch terminus.

1874 - Great Eastern Railway took over the operation of the long established ferry-boat service between North Greenwich and Greenwich itself.

1876 - Covered way opened at Shadwell, which gave passengers an interchange between the London & Blackwall system and the East London Railway.

1877 - New pier for ferries opened adjacent to North Greenwich station.

1880 (23rd Aug.) - First day of through locomotive working on Millwall Extension Railway.

1880 (5th April) - Limehouse Curve opened for freight traffic. Line also used for passengers 1/9/1880 - 1/3/1881, and also during the summer months of 1890 and 1891.

1888 - East & West India Docks Company amalgamated with the London & St. Katherines Dock Company to form the London & India Docks Joint Committee.

1890 (1st July) - North London services to Blackwall ceased. After this date, all trains were cut back to terminate at Poplar East India Road.

1892 (3rd April) - Last train from Fenchurch Street to Bow N.L.R.

1892 (4th April) - Covered way connection for passengers opened between the newly resited Bow Road station and Bow station on the North London Line.

1895 - 1896 - London & Blackwall viaduct between Fenchurch Street and Stepney again widened, this time to accommodate an additional down line.

1901 - Title of London & India Docks Joint Committee changed to London & India Docks Company.

1902 (2nd June) - Whitechapel & Bow Joint Railway opened from Campbell Road Junction, Bow to Whitechapel, to allow through running between the L.T. & S.R. and the Metropolitan District Railway, and therefore alleviate some of the overcrowding at Fenchurch Street.

1902 (4th Aug.) - Greenwich Foot Tunnel opened by L.C.C.

1902 (31st Oct.) - Railway ferry service from North Greenwich to Greenwich withdrawn.

1908 (4th Oct.) - Sunday trains between Stepney and Blackwall withdrawn.

1909 (1st Feb.) Responsibility for the operation of the North London system handed over to the London & North Western Railway.

1909 (31st Mar.) - Port of London Authority formed. This took over the administration of both the London & India Dock and the Millwall Dock Companies.

1912 (7th Aug.) Royal Assent given to Bill which authorised the take-over of the former London, Tilbury and Southend system by the Midland Railway.

1913 (28th Dec.) Sunday trains between Millwall Junction and North Greenwich withdrawn.

1917 - Closure of covered footway between Bow Road and Bow stations.

1923 (1st Jan.) The Railway Grouping, in which the majority of lines in Great Britain were amalgamated into four large companies. The organisations associated with the history of the L. & B. were absorbed thus:-

The Great Eastern and Great Northern systems were both absorbed by the London & North Eastern Railway, whilst the Midland and the London North Western systems became part of the London Midland & Scottish Railway.

1926 (4th May) - Blackwall and North Greenwich branches closed to passengers.

1946 - The abandoned station at Blackwall was demolished to provide a site for the new Brunswick Power Station.

1948 (1st Jan.) - The railways of Great Britain were nationalised, and became known as British Railways. The former Blackwall system was taken over by the Eastern Region, whilst the old L.T. & S.R. route beyond Gas Factory Junction, Bow, became Midland Region.

1949 (20th Feb.) - Former L.T. & S.R. line transferred from the Midland Region to the Eastern Region of British Railways.

1949 (7th Nov.) - Blackwall Extension Railway line between Gas Factory and Bow Junctions closed to regular passenger traffic.

1951 (14th April) - Special railtour formed last train over the section of line between Stepney Junction and Limehouse. After this, the points at the west end were disconnected.

1962 (17th June) - Inauguration of full electric services from Fenchurch Street to Southend etc.

1963 (10th May) - Limehouse Curve officially abandoned, and points removed at Salmons Lane Junction. This line had been out of use since 5/11/1962.

1966 - Remainder of Stepney - Brunswick Junction (Poplar) and Millwall Jct. - Millwall Docks sections officially abandoned. These lines had been little used since regular traffic ceased around 1962.

1967 (29th Dec.) - Total closure of line from Gas Factory Junction to Bow, North London.

1982 (Dec) - Government approval given to reopening of line between Stepney and Poplar, as part of the new Docklands Light Railway.

1987 (30th July) - Docklands Light Railway officially opened by H.M.the Queen.Public services did not begin immediately due to technical difficulties.

1987 (31st August) - Docklands Light Railway opened to the public.

NOTE:
Information on the opening and closure dates of individual stations and goods depots can be found in Appendices Two, Three and Four.

Appendix Two

PASSENGER STATIONS OPENINGS AND CLOSURES

	OPENED	CLOSED	NOTES
Blackwall	6.7.1840	4.5.1926	
Bow & Bromley	2.4.1849	26.9.1850	
Bow Road (Original Station)	1.10.1876	4.4.1892	1
Bow Road (Second Station)	4.4.1892	7.11.1949	2
Burdett Road	11.9.1871	21.4.1941	3
Cannon-street Road	21.8.1842	c.Nov or Dec.1848	
Fenchurch Street	2.8.1841	—	
Leman Street	1.6.1877	7.7.1941	4
Limehouse	6.7.1840	4.5.1926	
Millwall Docks	18.12.1871	4.5.1926	5
Millwall Junction	18.12.1871	4.5.1926	
Minories	6.7.1840	24.10.1853	6
North Greenwich & Cubitt Town	29.7.1872	4.5.1926	
Poplar (Original station)	6.7.1840	c1845	7
Poplar (Second station)	c.1845	4.5.1926	

Shadwell	1.10.1840	7.7.1941	8
South Dock	18.12.1871	4.5.1926	
Stepney	c 3.8.1840	—	9
Victoria Park & Bow	2.4.1849	26.9.1850	10
West India Docks	6.7.1840	4.5.1926	

NOTES

1.
Replaced by new station opened the same day.

2.
Built to the north of its predecessor, and provided with a covered way interchange to Bow station on the North London Line until early 1917. Bow Road station temporarily closed 21.4.1941 - 9.12.1946, and 6.1.1947 - 6.10.1947.

3.
Temporarily closed for approx. one week from 29.12.1940 due to bomb damage. Probably fell into complete disuse after air-raid of 10.4.1941.

4.
Temporarily closed 22.5.1916 - 1.7.1919.

5.
Name sometimes shown as Millwall Docks (Glengall Road).

6.
Temporarily closed 15th February - 9th September 1849.

7.
Replaced same day by new station slightly east of original.

8.
Renamed Shadwell & St. Georges East 1.7.1900: Temporarily closed 22.5.1916 - 5.5.1919.

9.
Renamed Stepney East 1.7.1923: Blackwall line platforms closed 4.5.1926: Renamed Limehouse 11.5.1987.

10.
Eastern Counties Railway platforms remained open until 6.1.1851.

PLEASE NOTE: Details of Docklands Light Railway stations can be found in **Appendix Three.**

Appendix Three

DOCKLANDS LIGHT RAILWAY STATIONS

Unless shown otherwise, all stations opened to passenger traffic along with the system on Monday 31.8.87. A formal Royal opening of the line had taken place a month earlier on 30.7.87., but public services were not introduced until various operational problems had been resolved.

CURRENT NAME	PROPOSED NAMES(S)	NOTES
ALL SAINTS CHRISP STREET MARKET	East India Dock Road/ Poplar High Street.	
BOW CHURCH	Bow Road	
CANARY WHARF	Canary Quay	1
CARMEN STREET	Fawe Street	2
CROSSHARBOUR	Glengall Grove	
DEVONS ROAD		
HERON QUAYS	Heron Wharf	
ISLAND GARDENS	Greenwich North/ Cubitt Town	
LIMEHOUSE	Stepney East	
MUDCHUTE	Millwall Park/ East Ferry Road	
POPLAR		3
PUDDING MILL LANE	Marshgate Lane	2
SHADWELL		

SOUTH QUAY	Cuba Street	
STRATFORD		4
TOWER GATEWAY	Minories Tower Hill	
WESTFERRY	West Ferry Road/ Limehouse.	
WEST INDIA QUAY	North Quay/ West India Dock.	

NOTES:

1.
Initially built to standard D.L.R. pattern. but dismantled during August/early September 1987 to make way for much larger structure. Station will open at a later date.

2.
To be opened later when funding permits.

3.
Referred to on early maps and diagrams etc. simply as 'Depot' or 'Interchange'.

4.
D.L.R. services utilise Platform Four at the existing station, therefore allowing convenient interchange with both British Rail and L.R.T. Central Line.

PLEASE NOTE:

For the sake of completeness, all D.L.R. stations have been listed, regardless of whether they are situated on the former L. & B. route.

Appendix Four

OPENING AND CLOSURES OF GOODS DEPOTS

	COMPANY	OPENED	CLOSED	NOTES
City Goods	M.R.	1.10.1862	1.7.1949	
Commercial Road	L.T.&S.R.	17.4.1886	3.7.1967	
East India Dock	L.& B.	1859	c.1961	
East India Dock	G.N.R.	c.1870	c.1961	
East Smithfield	G.E.R.	17.6.1864	1.9.1966	1
Goodmans Yard	L & B	1.2.1861	1.4.1951	2
Haydon Square	L.N.W.R.	2.1853	2.7.1962	
Minories	L. & B.	c.1842	c.1849	
Mint Street	L. & B.	1.8.1858	1.4.1951	3
Poplar	L. & B.	c.1842	c.1849	
Poplar Dock	M.R.	1.12.1882	4.5.1956	4
West India Docks	L. & B.	c.1842	c.1849	

NOTES

1.
Line extended onto dock premises, and depot renamed East Smithfield, London Docks, 1.9.1865.

2.
Built to cater for the needs of the E.C.R. and L.T. & S.R.

3.
Known for the first month or so as 'Minories'. Leased to the G.N.R. from 1.2.1861. Renamed Royal Mint St. c.1870.

4.
Renamed Poplar Dock Riverside 1.1951.

KEY TO RAILWAY COMPANY INITIALS

E.C.R.	Eastern Counties Railway
G.E.R.	Great Eastern Railway
G.N.R.	Great Northern Railway
L. & B.	London & Blackwall Railway
L.N.W.R.	London & North Western Railway
L.T. & S.R.	London Tilbury & Southend Railway
M.R.	Midland Railway

Appendix Five

LONDON & BLACKWALL RAILWAY LOCOMOTIVES PRIOR TO 1866

JONES & POTTS CLASS 2-2-2WT

Total weight: Around 22 tons. Cylinders: 13½" x 18"**
Driving Wheels: 5'6". Leading & Trailing Wheels: 3'6".

Works No.	Running No.	Name	Built	Renumbered 1866	Renumbered 1878	Withdrawn
281	1	Stepney	1848	91	910	10/1880
282	2	Shadwell	1848	92	920	4/1882
283	3	Blackwall	1848	93	930	4/1883
284	4	London	1848	95	-	4/1873
285	5	Bow	1848	96	960	10/1880
286	6	Thames	1848	97	-	11/1875*

NOTES

** *Later changed to 14" x 20" as follows: Nos. 2,3,4, and 6 in 1864: Nos. 1 and 5 in 1865.*

* *Withdrawn from G.E.R. stock after this date, and transferred to Millwall Extension Railway. Finally scrapped c.1880.*

GEORGE ENGLAND CLASS SMALL 2-2-2WT

Total Weight: 13 tons. Cylinders: 9" x 12".
Driving Wheels: 4'6". Leading & Trailing Wheels: 3'.

Name	Built	Withdrawn
Dwarf	9/1849	1852*
Pygmy Giant	1/1850	1852**

NOTES

* *Re-sold by George England & Co. Ltd. to the L.N.W.R. in 1853 for use in their Permanent Way Dept. Probably scrapped c.1863.*

** *Re-sold by George England & Co. Ltd. to Sandy & Potton Railway in 1857, where it was renamed 'Little England'. Taken over by Bedford & Cambridge Railway in 1862, and sold the following year to the L.& N.W.R. who further re-named it 'Dwarf', and used it as a replacement for the original engine of the same name. Actual date of scrapping unknown.*

JONES & POTTS CLASS IMPROVED 2-2-2WT

Total Weight: Around 22 tons. Cylinders: 15" x 18".
Driving Wheels: 5'6". Leading & Trailing Wheels: 3'6".

Works No.	Running No.	Name	Built	Renumbered 1866	Renumbered 1878	Withdrawn
292	7	Victoria	1850	98	980	8/1880

GEORGE ENGLAND CLASS 2-2-2WT

Total Weight: Around 22 tons. Cylinders: 15" x 18".
Driving Wheels: 5'6". Leading & Trailing Wheels: 3'6".

Works No.	Running No.	Name	Built	Renumbered 1866	Renumbered 1878	Withdrawn
?	8	Samson	1852	99	990	10/1881
?	9	Hercules	1852	100	-	4/1870*

* *Last used 6/1866*

GEORGE ENGLAND CLASS 2-4-0T GOODS ENGINES

Total Weight Unknown. Cylinders: 15" x 22".
Driving Wheels: 4'. Leading Wheels: 3'.

Works No.	Running No.	Built	Renumbered 1866	Renumbered 1878	Withdrawn
?	10	1860	101	1010	1/1882
?	11	1860	102	1020	2/1882

Select Bibliography Of Printed Sources

During the production of this book, the following publications have been consulted, and all of them make excellent further reading for those interested in the history of London's Railways:

All Stations to Poplar,J.E.Connor (Connor & Butler)

Chronology of London Railways H.V.Borley (Railway & Canal History Society)

Docklands Light Railway: A Journey Through History. Three leaflets (D.L.R.)

Docklands Light Railway Official Handbook. Stephen Jolly and Bob Bayman (Capital Transport)

First & Last Loves. John Betjeman (Murray)

Great Eastern Railway Society Information Sheet No. P116: O.S. Plans Fenchurch Street to Blackwall & North Greenwich. D.J.Taylor.

Liverpool Street – Shenfield Electrification. George Dow (British Railways)

Locomotive Magazine. Various issues.

Loco Profiles – No. 27 'The Tilbury Tanks' (Profile Publications)

London Railways. Edwin Course (Batsford)

London's Historic Railway Stations. John Betjeman & John Gay (Murray)

London's Industrial Archaeology: No.2. 1980 (GLIAS Periodical)

London's Local Railways. Alan A. Jackson (David & Charles)

London's Lost Railways. Charles Klapper (Routledge Keagan Paul)

London's Termini. Alan A. Jackson (David & Charles)

Memories of Old Poplar. John Blake (Stepney Books)

Modern Railways. January 1984.

P.L.A. Railways. T.B.Peacock (Locomotive Publishing Co.)

The Blackwall & Millwall Extension Railways. Geoffrey Body (Avon Anglia)

The Co-partnership Herald. Nov. 1936 (Commercial Gas Company Periodical)

The East London Line and the Thames Tunnel. Charles E.Lee. (L.T.)

The Great Eastern Railway) Cecil J. Allen (Ian Allan)

The London Tilbury & Southend Railway.H.D.Welch (Oakwood)

The P.L.A. Monthly. April 1938 (Periodical)

The North London Railway. Michael Robbins (Oakwood)

The Railway Magazine. Various issues, but particularly Vol.LX (May 1927)

The Railways of Great Britain and Ireland,1842 Whishaw

100 Years of the District. Charles E. Lee (London Transport)

Plus numerous documents, pamphlets and press cuttings which are held in the Local Studies Department, Central Library, Bancroft Road, London E.1.

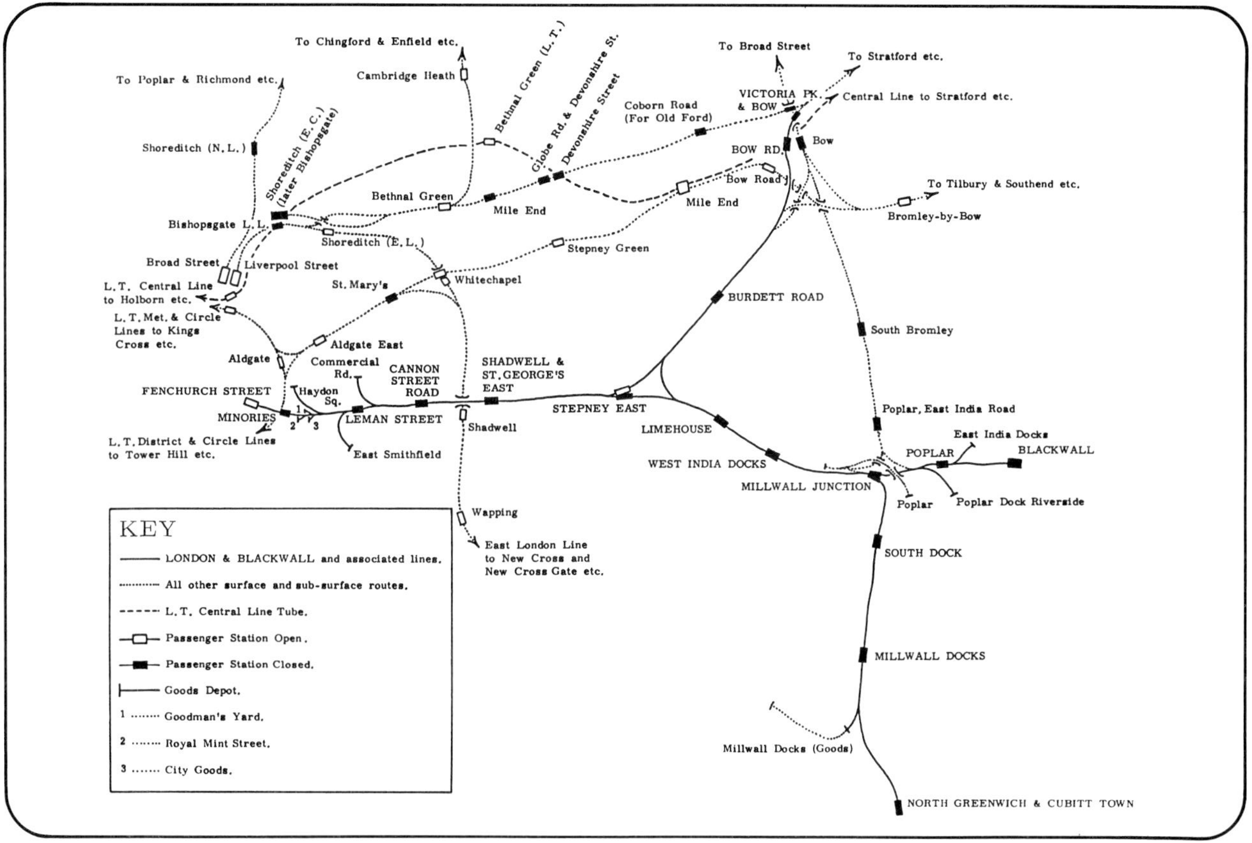

THE RAILWAYS OF TOWER HAMLETS
(Prior to the construction of the Docklands Light Railway)